A Teaching Assistant's Guide to Managing Behaviour in the Classroom

Challenging behaviour amongst pupils is as much of a headache for teaching assistants as it is for teachers. This book, specifically written with teaching assistants in mind, looks at common behaviour problems in the classroom, explains typical causes of misbehaviour and shows what teaching assistants can do to tackle and tame disruptive students in their care. Using a range of case studies, all of which reflect real-life situations and discussed from the perspective of a teaching assistant, Susan Bentham explores:

- the role of the teaching assistant in relation to School Behaviour Policies
- when and how to reward good behaviour
- how understanding the reasons for disruptive behaviour can help to determine the most appropriate way of dealing with it
- how to implement behaviour strategies that really work.

Mirroring the course content of most Teaching Assistant GNVQ and Foundation degree qualifications, the author adopts a reflective approach to behaviour management. She effectively illustrates how practitioners can learn from their experiences and develop new skills and coping strategies, which will enable them to concentrate on the most important part of their job: supporting learning.

This book is a must-buy for any teaching assistant for whom bad behaviour is proving to be their biggest everyday challenge.

Susan Bentham teaches Psychology at Bognor Regis Adult Education Centre, West Sussex.

A Teaching Assistant's Guide to Managing Behaviour in the Classroom

Susan Bentham

 Routledge
Taylor & Francis Group

LONDON AND NEW YORK

First published 2006 by Routledge
2 Park Square, Milton Park, Abingdon, Oxon OX14 4RN

Simultaneously published in the USA and Canada
by Routledge
270 Madison Ave, New York, NY 10016

Routledge is an imprint of the Taylor & Francis Group

© 2006 Susan Bentham

Typeset in Sabon by
Keystroke, Jacaranda Lodge, Wolverhampton
Printed and bound in Great Britain by
Bell & Bain Ltd, Glasgow

British Library Cataloguing in Publication Data
A catalogue record for this book is available from the British Library

Library of Congress Cataloging in Publication Data
Bentham, Susan, 1958–
A teaching assistant's guide to managing behaviour in the classroom /
Susan Bentham.–1st ed.
p. cm.
Includes bibliographical references and index.
ISBN 0–415–35119–7 (pbk. : alk. paper)
1. Classroom Management–United States–Handbooks, manuals, etc.
2. School children–United States–Discipline–Handbooks, manuals,
etc. 3. Teachers' assistants–United States–Handbooks, manuals, etc.
I. Title.
LB3013.B397 2005
371.102'4.–dc22   2005005248

ISBN 0–415–35119–7

To my sons, Matthew and Bobby

Contents

Acknowledgements

Susan Bentham would like to thank all her students, past and present, for their timely comments and suggestions. This book would not have been possible without them.

Introduction

This book was written for teaching assistants and aims to offer practical advice on how to handle everyday behaviour problems. As such it is hoped that this book will be a valuable resource for those teaching assistants enrolled on courses to include: NVQ 2 and 3, HLTA award and Foundation degrees. In addition it is hoped that tutors involved in such programmes will find this book to be an extremely useful teaching tool.

This book looks at ways of dealing with students who:

- are never in their seats
- disrupt other students
- continually talk out of turn
- use inappropriate language
- refuse to do what is asked of them
- have difficulty in controlling anger.

The first key point to stress is that dealing with behavioural problems is the responsibility of all those who are working within the school. A teaching assistant has a vital role to play in regard to encouraging appropriate behaviour and dealing with inappropriate behaviour. However, a teaching assistant does not work in isolation and at all times needs to provide feedback to and take advice from teachers and other members of staff.

When discussing difficulties in dealing with behaviour, it is human nature to want to find easy solutions – 'just tell me what to do'. However, this book argues that behaviour is complex. There can be a number of reasons why a student misbehaves as well as a number of strategies that could be used to deal with the behaviour.

This book offers guidance by outlining a number of tools that a teaching assistant can use to make sense of the behaviour and to develop coping strategies.

These tools include:

- knowledge

    - of roles and responsibilities within the school's behaviour policy,
    - of theoretical explanations of behaviour,
    - of specific strategies to deal with problem behaviour,

- ways of recording the details of specific incidents,
- ways of questioning or reflecting on what happened, to include strategies that were employed, what worked, what didn't work and how to improve on current practice.

In discussing and offering guidance on behaviour this book uses many case studies. The case studies describe everyday situations that a teaching assistant could encounter at either primary or secondary level. Although explanations of the behaviours illustrated in the case studies are given and various strategies are put forward, this book does not suggest that these are the only explanations for the behaviour or the only strategies that can be used.

Essentially, the case studies are designed to encourage teaching assistants to think about what happens within the classroom. In this regard it is hoped that the case studies will serve as a useful learning device. In dealing with problem behaviour there are no easy solutions, for behaviour, like life, can be complicated and messy.

Chapter 1

The role of the teaching assistant in managing behaviour

A collegiate approach

It was all a bit of a shock really. It was my first week as a teaching assistant. The class had just divided into small groups to do a writing exercise. The teacher and I were moving around the class to check that all students were on task. The noise was very loud at times and the teacher had to remind the groups to settle down. I noticed that the teacher at times had to struggle to make herself heard. Group discussion is now seen as positive, though I noticed that as I went round the class some of the groups were discussing everything but what they were supposed to.

There was one student who was cutting up little pieces of paper, crumpling them up and throwing them in the wastepaper bin. Sometimes he missed and hit some of the girls sitting at the next table. The teacher told him to stop; he did for a while, then when her back was turned he again started crumpling up bits of paper, though I must admit that at least he was not throwing them anymore. At one point there looked like there was going to be a fight between two boys. One boy got out of his seat and wandered over to the other boy and said there was a nasty smell in the class. The other boy obviously took offence to this and stood up, clenched his fists and asked the other boy if he wanted to repeat what he had said. The teacher intervened at that point, though I don't think she heard what started it, and asked both boys to return to their seats and get back to work. At break the teacher commented that she thought the previous session had gone fairly well. I just smiled and agreed.

As a teaching assistant I realised that I had a role in making sure that students behaved but I was not exactly sure about what my role was.

What could I do or say?

Could I ask the class to be quiet? I noticed one of the senior teaching assistants do this. But if I asked the class to be quiet would I be overstepping my role?

Did the teacher hear what had started that argument between those two boys? Should I have told the teacher that the student had started throwing crumpled-up paper again?

Should I have dealt with it? How could I have dealt with it?

Did I need permission from the teacher to do this?

Would the students listen to me?

This chapter examines a teaching assistant's role in managing classroom behaviour. The first point to make is that promoting positive behaviour is everyone's responsibility. When everyone in the school takes responsibility for behaviour the school is said to be taking a 'collegiate approach' to managing behaviour. What the above case study illustrates is that for a collegiate approach to work, everyone involved must understand their roles and responsibilities and those of others. Issues concerning what is acceptable and unacceptable behaviour and systems of rewards and reprimands need to be discussed.

From a teacher's perspective:

- a teaching assistant can provide support in keeping students on task;
- a teaching assistant can keep an eye on the class if the teacher is busy working with an individual or a small group;
- a teaching assistant can act as a second pair of eyes and give the teacher valuable information about what is happening in the classroom;
- a teaching assistant can observe students' behaviour and fill in relevant records.

From the teaching assistants' perspective:

- teaching assistants need to know what rewards and reprimands they can hand out themselves and which they must negotiate or check with the teacher first;
- for teaching assistants to do their job effectively, students need to respect their authority
- teaching assistants need guidance from the teacher. They need to know whether they were right in their handling of a situation.

However, both teachers and teaching assistants need each other's support, encouragement and praise. Teachers and teaching assistants need time to talk to each other about behavioural issues. In a sense, it is not only 'good to talk' it is *essential* to talk.

The behaviour policy

Every school will have numerous policies that deal with behaviour. Most policies are based on rights and responsibilities.

Rights	Responsibilities
To be respected	Respect others
Not to be bullied	Not to bully others. Report incidents of bullying
To feel safe	To behave in a reasonable manner that ensures the safety of others
To receive a good education	To listen to others
To be able to work without interference	To accept support To come prepared for lessons To behave appropriately so others can learn
To work in a pleasant environment	To respect the environment

The school in which you work will have a behaviour/discipline policy, home–school agreements, school charters, an anti-bullying policy and policies on equal opportunities. As a teaching assistant you will need to be familiar with these, in particular your role and the role of others within these policies.

What follows is an example of a behaviour policy following guidance from the Department for Education and Skills (2002).

Behaviour policy of Everytown Primary School

Rationale

This policy aims to create a positive learning environment where there is mutual cooperation, respect and trust. We will reinforce behaviours that exemplify the values of fairness, honesty and consideration. As a school we believe that all positive behaviour should be rewarded and that inappropriate behaviour is dealt with firmly and fairly.

Purpose

- To have a whole-school approach to good behaviour that is implemented consistently across the school by all staff to include teachers, supply teachers, teaching assistants and lunch-time supervisors.
- To use praise to encourage cooperation and consideration.
- To use those students who do behave well as positive role models for other students.
- When reprimanding a student's behaviour to make a distinction between the child and their behaviour. The child's behaviour is being punished as opposed to the child.
- To communicate with and involve parents/carers in any concerns regarding the children's behaviour. Parents and carers have their role to play in helping to create a learning environment where there is mutual cooperation, respect and trust.
- To develop within children an understanding that there are consequences for their chosen behaviour.
- To ensure that there is equality of opportunity and that there is provision to meet educational, social and behavioural needs of children.
- The school will not tolerate any form of bullying. All allegations will be taken seriously and promptly dealt with.

Approach to children

- Listen to and respect children's views.
- Talk to children calmly.
- Be approachable.
- Be fair and consistent.
- Provide clear boundaries of what is acceptable and what is non-acceptable behaviour.
- Be positive.
- Give lots of praise for good behaviour.
- When reprimanding bad behaviour, focus on the behaviour, not the child.
- Build upon what the child can do.
- Never use humiliation.
- Help children to accept and learn from their mistakes.
- Help children to take responsibility for their behaviour.

School rules

- Be courteous and considerate at all times.
- Take responsibility for your own actions.
- Respect the rights and beliefs of others.
- Follow instructions.
- Look after equipment and keep things tidy.
- Be respectful of your own and others' property.
- Walk quietly around the school.
- Keep the school clean and tidy.

Rewards

- Praise, both non-verbal and verbal, needs to be sincere. The child needs to be told specifically what behaviour they are being rewarded for.
- Smiley faces, stars and house-points.
- As part of every Friday's assembly two children from each class are chosen for a special mention. They will have their names written in the Golden Book and be given a special sticker to take home.

Sanctions

Our school divides unacceptable behaviour into the following.

Level One: here misbehaviour will be effectively managed within the classroom by strategies such as rule reminders, giving a choice, warning of consequences, missing playtime, in-class time out and out-of-class time out.

Level Two: more serious misbehaviour (i.e. minor vandalism, threatening behaviour, bullying, isolated acts of violence) that can not be managed within a classroom will involve notification and involvement of other staff to include the head teacher. At this stage the student's name will be entered into the behaviour book. At this point the class teacher may involve the parents.

Level Three: very serious episodes of misbehaviour (i.e. vandalism of school property, leaving school premises without consent, aggressive behaviour causing deliberate injury) or persistent level two misbehaviour will necessitate the involvement of the head teacher and parents. It is possible at this point that outside agencies such as the education welfare service and the behaviour support team will be involved.

Severe clause: in the event of persistent unacceptable behaviour and where other strategies and sanctions have not worked the school will follow the Exclusions – Good Practice Guidelines.

Supporting children who find it difficult to manage their behaviour

Some children will be identified as having 'behavioural special needs'. The school, acting in consultation with the parents of the child concerned and where necessary outside agencies, will draw up a behaviour plan. The behaviour plan aims to produce improvement in the child's behaviour over a specified period of time. At this school, the Special Educational Needs Coordinator (SENCO) runs a chill-out room, where children who have behaviour problems can go to for time out and support. In addition, the SENCO runs specific programmes to develop social skills. While the behaviour of children with 'behavioural special needs' will be dealt with sympathetically and sensitively, unacceptable behaviour will not go unchallenged.

(DfES 2002)

The above example of a behaviour policy is a composite of many behaviour policies. It is a shortened version and many policies will include more details regarding the specific roles of teachers, head teachers, SENCOs, governors and various intervention strategies to use. There will be similarities as well as differences in regard to school policies at a secondary level. As a teaching assistant it is important that you become familiar with your school's behaviour policy and you will need to discuss with members of your school, i.e. teachers, SENCO, what your specific role involves.

Some examples of comments from teaching assistants follow.

I always use praise to reward good behaviour. As a teaching assistant I can give out stickers for good work, trying hard and behaving well. I can also give out team points or recommend a child for a team point. The teacher can give out special rewards such as entering the child's name into the Golden Book. When a child is not behaving, I will try to deal with the situation first. If I think the behaviour is serious enough I can remove or recommend that the teacher remove a house-point. I can also put a child's name on the board and can keep a child back for a few minutes at playtime. However, only the teacher can remove a playtime, enter the child's name into the behaviour log, take the child to the head teacher and talk to the parents.

I work in a secondary school and I write reports on the students' behaviour. If a student works well I will fill in a commendation form; likewise if they have been misbehaving I will write a referral. The teacher, on the basis of the referral note, will discuss with the student their behaviour at the end of the lesson. If the teacher sees fit they will set a detention. Referral notes are an important ongoing record of the student's behaviour.

I work as a teaching assistant in a secondary school attached to the Science department. When we started school this year, the Department Head introduced me to the class and said that I was there to help him support students in his class. He told the class that I was acting on his behalf and if the students disobeyed me that they would have to answer to him. I really appreciated his comments and have felt that the students respect my authority.

Activity

The aim of the following activity is to help clarify your role within the school with regard to behaviour. The activity looks at daily routines in terms of appropriate behaviour that is expected from students. Once you have outlined how the students are expected to behave, then you need to say what you would do if they did not behave accordingly.

What is appropriate behaviour?

Routine	Students are expected to:	A teaching assistant will intervene when:	A teaching assistant will inform the teacher if:
• In the playground			
• Standing outside in the corridor waiting to come into the class			
• When entering the class			

continued

Routine	Students are expected to:	A teaching assistant will intervene when:	A teaching assistant will inform the teacher if:
• Where to sit			
• When wishing to participate in class			
• When coming into the class late			
• When requesting help			
• When working in groups			
• When it is time to leave the classroom			

Outside support agencies

Schools do not work in isolation but will have support from various agencies. The following outlines of the roles of the major support teams are drawn from the West Sussex Behaviour Guidance (2000). *The behaviour support team* will be involved with primary schools, working alongside teachers in the planning and implementation of behavioural programmes for specific students. The team will also participate in school-based initiatives for primary and secondary schools.

The looked after children team provides educational support to children who are looked after by the authority, that is, children who are in children's homes or foster care. This team work with staff within the school to implement a personal education plan that aims to raise educational standards.

The traveller education support service seeks to inform schools of the social and cultural traditions of this group in order to encourage understanding and to help schools deal with any potential disadvantage faced by such students. Lack of an understanding of the culture of travellers may put such children at a greater risk of prejudice and bullying.

The support team for ethnic minority pupils deals with any potential problems that might occur due to interaction between different cultures. The team will give support regarding learning English as a second language, supporting bilingual learners and offering training on refugees and asylum seekers and welcoming new arrivals.

The educational psychology service, primarily educational psychologists, uses specific knowledge of educational and psychological theory to support schools. In particular, team members aim to advise schools on practical strategies that can be used to help students to behave in a suitable manner.

The educational welfare service is concerned with promoting regular school attendance. This service is involved with students whose non-attendance may be due to emotional and behavioural difficulties.

Behaviour targets and behaviour plans

Students with specific behavioural problems (associated with conditions such as attention deficit hyperactivity disorder (ADHD) or autistic spectrum disorder (ASD) or students who consistently display more serious misbehaviour will often have their own behaviour plans or have behaviour targets written on an Individual Educational Plan (IEP). A behaviour plan will outline the nature of the difficulty, a small number of targets to be achieved, resources available, strategies to be used, details of how progress will be monitored and a date for review.

All targets should be *S.M.A.R.T.*:

Specific: Observable and precise description of behaviour.

Measurable: Refers to the number of times (frequency) a behaviour occurs and how long a behaviour goes on for (duration). A target will include details of desired levels of behaviour.

Achievable: The student should have the ability to meet the target.

Relevant: Targets need to be related to the specific behavioural needs of the student.

Time-limited: A realistic and appropriate time frame is given for the student to achieve the target.

Case study

In the following case study, Jane, a teaching assistant in a junior school, describes Rory Smith. Rory is determined always to have his own way. Rory can be charming when things are going the way he wants, but when he has to do something he does not want to do then there is trouble. Rory can be very threatening to other students and his language is a matter of concern. Rory has a behaviour plan.

Behaviour plan

Name: RS

Area of concern: Intimidating behaviour and inappropriate language

Year Group: 4

Class teacher: Mrs Todd   Review date:

Support by: JW (teaching assistant)   Support began:

Targets to be achieved	Achievement criteria	Possible resources or techniques	Possible class strategies	Ideas for teaching assistant	Outcome
To interact with others without threatening or intimidating them.	Reduced number of incidents in a 12 week period. In the previous 12-week period there were 20 incidents that were recorded in the Red Book.	School policy on bullying. Loss of playground time. Name in Red Book. Social skills input.	Intervene early. Remind student of consequences. Praise efforts towards achieving targets. Keep a record of behaviour.	All of previous. Talk about any incidents that have occurred. Help student to reflect on other ways he could have behaved. What could he have done? Keep a record of behaviour.	
To use appropriate and respectful language.	No bad language over a 12-week period.	Consistent reminders that swearing is not permitted. Praise for appropriate language. Loss of playground time for episodes of swearing.	Remind about rules. Give praise and attention for controlling inappropriate language. Keep a record of behaviour.	Discuss what language is appropriate and why. Discuss alternative strategies for bad language. Keep a record of behaviour.	

The role of a teaching assistant

The role of a teaching assistant (TA) is to help students achieve their targets. Teaching assistants will use the strategies suggested on their behaviour plan and keep records of the student's behaviour. These records will assist the teacher and SENCO in deciding whether the strategies that have been used have been successful. The following example details Jane's notes on Rory's behaviour.

> After the class science experiment I asked Rory to help me tidy up. Rory mumbled something under his breath. I reminded Rory that it was school policy to be helpful and to talk to each other with respect. I told him that he knew that the consequence for using inappropriate language was to miss break and that he should think carefully about what he should say. I also reminded Rory that when we were feeling like we might say something we shouldn't, we should try to count up to ten slowly and think nice thoughts. Rory just glared at me and said 'Tidy up yourself, you f*****g cow!' I followed the agreed strategy. I calmly told him that such language was not appropriate and that, as he knew, the consequence was that he would miss afternoon break. Rory told me that he 'didn't f*** care' as he was already missing afternoon break. I didn't say anything to him, but referred the incident to the supply teacher. Usually the threat of missing playtime keeps Rory in line, but I have noticed that when he knows he has already lost that privilege, his behaviour just goes to pieces and becomes impossible to control.

In this short write-up Jane includes important observations regarding the effectiveness of strategies being used. Jane needs to communicate these observations to the teacher. Jane's observation that threatening to withdraw a privilege, in this case playtime, is no longer effective in controlling behaviour when the student has already lost that privilege will aid the teacher and SENCO in determining whether the existing strategies for dealing with Rory's behaviour are working or whether they need to be altered.

Summary

In this short chapter we have looked at behaviour policies and behaviour plans specifically focusing on the role of the teaching assistant. However, behaviour is everyone's responsibility.

Chapter 2

Explanations and strategies

Introduction

Often, when talking to teaching assistants about behaviour in the class, they will describe situations which they found difficult to deal with, for example, how the group they were working with would not settle or how a student would simply not do what they were told. What they want to know is what can they do to improve the situation? What can they do to prevent students from arguing? How can they feel more confident when working with students?

As described in Chapter 1, teaching assistants will work with other members of the school, specifically the teacher, in implementing the behaviour policy. Teaching assistants will need to know how their school defines acceptable and unacceptable behaviour and they will need to understand their role within the school's behaviour policy. Most importantly, teaching assistants will need to talk continually to teachers regarding how they deal with students who misbehave. Managing behaviour is everyone's responsibility!

A vast amount of information will be presented within this chapter. This information aims to explain both the reasons behind inappropriate behaviour and the possible strategies that can be used to turn behaviour around. The first point to make is the connection between strategies and explanations.

Simply put, this means that if we can understand why the students are behaving in such a way (what are the explanations for their behaviour) then we can work out what we can do to turn their behaviour around.

You might at this point be saying: 'So all I have to do is to figure out why the student or students are doing what they are doing and then I will know what to do?' At this point I will say 'yes, *but*'. Of course, when someone says '*but*', you know that things are going to get complicated, and behaviour is a complex issue.

Any behaviour can be explained by a number of causes. Let's look at the following example.

> Joe is in Year 2. He is supposed to be working on a maths worksheet. However, Joe is playing with an action doll that he has brought in from home. You have reminded him twice of the school rules that he has to keep his toys in his drawer during lesson time but he has ignored you.
>
> *Why is he doing this?*
>
> *What are the possible explanations for this behaviour?*

- Perhaps Joe is testing you. Do you really mean what you say? Can he get away with this behaviour with you? Has Joe got away with this behaviour in the past? Perhaps Joe is getting a lot of attention from the other children in the class.

If this is the case then Joe's behaviour can be explained by past *consequences*.

- Perhaps Joe is having an 'off' day. Maybe he is feeling upset and having his action doll with him makes him feel better.

If this is the case then Joe's *feelings or emotions* are behind his behaviour.

- Perhaps Joe thinks he is a bad boy. Perhaps he has been told off many times and has come to believe he is a bad boy and therefore he has decided that he is going to act like one.

Here we see how a person's *thoughts or thinking processes* can influence their behaviour.

Whatever the explanation, Joe still needs to put away his toy and start working on his maths sheet, assuming that this is a class rule. However, the explanation of why he is behaving in such a way will influence how you respond to Joe and the strategy you will use.

If Joe is doing what he is doing because of past *consequences*, that is if he has been rewarded in the past for this behaviour (i.e. he likes the attention of an audience), it might be best to have a quiet word with Joe away from the rest of the class (remove the reward).

If Joe is doing what he is doing because of his *feelings or emotions*, that is, Joe is feeling upset, then although he still needs to put away his toy he would also benefit from having the opportunity to talk about why he is feeling upset. It is doubtful that if Joe is feeling upset about something he will be able to concentrate on his worksheet.

If Joe is doing what he is doing because of his *thoughts or thinking processes*, that is, Joe thinks he is a bad boy, then this will need to be dealt with by a concerted effort within the school. You might get Joe to put away his toy for the moment, but if Joe's thought processes are not tackled then there will be further episodes to deal with.

What the above example shows is that there can be a number of possible reasons or explanations for any behaviour and a number of possible responses or strategies that can be used.

To summarise:

- behaviour can be determined by past *consequences*;
- behaviour can be determined by *feelings or emotions*;
- behaviour can be determined by *thoughts or thinking processes*.

The following three sections examine behaviour from these viewpoints.

Behaviour determined by consequences

Explanations

Behaviourists believe that the way people behave is determined by previous consequences. Simply put, if you have been rewarded for behaving in a certain manner in the past then you are more like to repeat that behaviour in the future. Likewise, if you have been punished for behaviour in the past then the chances are that you are unlikely to repeat that behaviour in the future. This viewpoint argues that as behaviour is determined by consequences then to change behaviour we need to change the consequences of the behaviour.

In schools much attention is given to rewards. There are rewards for good behaviour in the form of merits, house-points, stickers and praise. However, there are also rewards for inappropriate behaviour in the form of attention, peer approval, power, escape and revenge.

A behaviourist explanation seems very clear and straightforward. However, the explanation becomes complex when you realise that what is considered a punishment and what is considered a reward depends very much on the individual. Consider the following example.

Jody always talks out of turn in class, is never in her seat and can be downright rude to the teaching assistant and the teacher. Jody is often sent out of the class by the teacher. The teacher might think that he is punishing Jody by sending her out of the class to stand in the corridor. However, the teacher notes that during three out of five lessons Jody is out in the corridor.

So what is happening?

The behaviourist approach would say that there must be a reward for this ongoing behaviour.

From Jody's perspective she has escaped from a subject she dislikes. Jody knows she has difficulties in maths and does not want to be shown up as inadequate by all those who can do the work. Jody does not like the teacher as she feels he is always having a go at her. However, being in the corridor gives her the opportunity to talk to other students who happen to walk by. Jody enjoys making faces through the window in the door at the other students when the teacher is not looking.

The rewards for Jody's ongoing disruptive behaviour are clear.

On the other hand the teacher finds the class much more manageable to teach when Jody is not there.

So from a behaviourist explanation both the teacher and Jody are being rewarded for their respective behaviours, which are consequently reinforced.

Social learning theory

Behaviourists also believe that people can learn not only from being rewarded or punished themselves but by watching what happens to other people, specifically if other people are rewarded or punished for their behaviour. This approach is called social learning theory. Social learning theory states that we learn by imitation. The people we imitate are called role models. In order to imitate someone's behaviour there are a number of steps involved.

1   We need to pay attention to the behaviour.
2   We need to be able to remember the behaviour, as it might be some time before we are in a position to imitate the behaviour.
3   We need to have the physical motor skills to imitate the behaviour. If we wished to imitate someone leaping over a desk we would need the physical prowess to do so. Some individuals might need to practise.
4   We need to be motivated to imitate the behaviour. Motivation depends on both whether we think we can imitate the behaviour and whether we would want to. Whether we would want to imitate the behaviour depends on whether we see the consequences of the behaviour as rewarding or punishing.

Social learning theory states that individuals are more likely to imitate role models who are seen as similar to themselves, who have been rewarded for their behaviour and who have power or status. We will now return to the example of Jody.

All the students in the class are very familiar with Jody's antics. The question is, would any other students want to imitate Jody's behaviour. Amanda has certainly watched Jody and can describe in great detail what Jody does. Amanda could act like Jody but she chooses not to. Amanda likes the class teacher, she is good at the subject and Amanda would be horrified if the teacher sent her out of the class. Being sent out of the class for Amanda would be a punishment.

Laura, on the other hand, hates the subject and the teacher. Laura watches Jody constantly and knows exactly what she does. Laura looks up to Jody and would like to imitate her, but Laura sees herself as desperately shy and just couldn't do the things that Jody does, much as she would like to.

To recap, behaviourists believe that behaviour is determined by the consequences of previous behaviour. If we are rewarded or if we see someone else being rewarded for behaviour we are *more likely* to repeat or imitate that behaviour in the future. If we are punished or if we see someone else being punished for behaviour we are more likely *not* to want to repeat or imitate the behaviour. However, it is very important to remember that what is seen as punishment or reward depends very much on the individual. This explanation of behaviour states that if you want to change a person's behaviour then you need to change the consequences of their behaviour. This leads on to the next section where we will talk about strategies.

Strategies

ABC approach

In order to change a behaviour it is first important to discover why a person is behaving in such a way. This approach requires you to observe someone's behaviour and to categorise the behaviour into antecedent (what happens before), behaviour (what they do) and consequence (what happens to the person as a result of their behaviour). Let's look at the example of Jody within this framework.

	Antecedent	Behaviour	Consequence
10:25	The rest of the class have started the maths worksheet and are on question 4. Jody has not begun the worksheet.	Jody is looking at everyone else working.	
10:30	The teacher calls out: 'Jody! Haven't you started yet? What are you waiting for? Christmas! I don't want any of your nonsense today.'	Jody glares at the teacher.	
10:32	TA approaches and asks if Jody needs any help to get started.	Jody looks up and notices that the other students are now all looking at her. Jody pushes her papers off her desk and yells: 'This is a f***** useless class!'	The teacher replies: 'I told you Jody, I will have none of your nonsense – out of the class'.
10:36		Jody is now standing outside in the corridor, smirking.	
10:37		Jody is having a chat with Joe, another student who is passing.	Joe says he will call her tonight.

continued

	Antecedent	Behaviour	Consequence
10:39		Jody is making faces at the other students through the window on the door.	The other students are smiling and trying hard not to giggle.

A structured observation, recording antecedent, behaviour and consequence is helpful in trying to figure out the reasons for a student's behaviour. It is important when carrying out such an observation to be objective and just record what you actually see and not what you think is going on. If we were to interpret this structured observation we could say that Jody's behaviour is being triggered by her inability to do the work, that her behaviour is being rewarded by escaping a situation which she does not like and reinforced by approval from others. There are several possible ways forward.

Create learning environments that are productive

If students are interested in what they are doing and if they feel that they can succeed then they are less likely to have behavioural problems. Lorenz (2001) talks of work being set at varying levels as detailed below.

Instructional level: Where the student can do approximately 95 per cent of the work by themselves. The student will need support on the other 5 per cent, but this will stretch them.

Independent level: Where the student can do approximately 99 per cent of the work by themselves. The problem with this is that the student can become bored.

Frustration level: Where the student can do less than 95 per cent of the work. If the student feels that the work set is too much of a struggle then the temptation is to give up and there is a risk that the student will start to behave disruptively.

As a teaching assistant, you have detailed knowledge of what a student can or cannot do. It is important to tell the teacher if you think the work set is just too difficult for the student you are supporting. In this way you can possibly prevent problems before they happen.

In the case study on Jody, having work that is set at the appropriate level would hopefully lead to Jody experiencing success. If Jody felt that she could do the work then maybe she would not have to behave disruptively.

'Catching them when they are good'

Often, what happens in the classroom is that when a student is behaving well, they are ignored. It is only when the student misbehaves that they get attention and any attention is better than none. It is important to reward students when they are behaving well, that is, 'catching them when they are good'.

However, with some students this can prove rather difficult. Sometimes a student never works sensibly on a task, never sits in a seat without fidgeting and never finishes a set task. In this case, one approach to changing behaviour is to ignore the minor misbehaviour if possible and to reward any behaviour that is appropriate. To begin with you might praise a student for just sitting at their desk quietly, but over time you might expect more and more from them, for example leading up to sitting quietly at their desk and working.

In the case study on Jody, you, as the teaching assistant, might notice Jody sitting at her desk, looking at her worksheet. You could go up to her and say: 'Jody I can see you are really trying to concentrate on the work that the teacher has set'. However, this strategy would only be effective if the work set was within her capabilities. So in a sense what we are seeing is that to really tackle unacceptable behaviour you need to use a combination of approaches.

Use praise

Praise is a very powerful reward, but there are a few points to consider regarding praise.

- Praise must be genuine and seen as such by the person receiving it. It is important to praise effort as well as achievement.
- Praise needs to be specific, that is, the person you are praising needs to know that you are praising them.
- Praise, to be effective, should be informative. It is important to say to the student 'well done', but it is equally important that the student knows why they have done well. In this way they can repeat the behaviour.

An issue regarding praise and giving rewards such as stickers and house-points is perceived fairness. Consider how you would handle the following comment from a very able student.

It's just not fair! Sam always mucks about in class. The teacher is always telling him off. But Sam only has to hand in a page with a few lines scribbled on it and he gets lots of praise, house-points, you name it. I sit in class, I always behave, and I never have to be told off. I spend a lot of time on my work. I can write pages. But I never get as many house-points as Sam does.

Language should be positive

It is very important for teaching assistants to be aware of the language that they use to students. Wherever possible comments and requests should be expressed in a positive manner. A teaching assistant should try to avoid using words such as: 'Don't', 'No', 'Stop'. For example:

'Don't lean back on the chair like that'

could be rephrased as

'Sam, we have a rule in this class for sitting correctly – thanks'.

Teachers and teaching assistants should avoid language that involves:

Labelling:	'People like you will never amount to anything.'
Comparison:	'You will never be as good as your sister.'
Sarcasm:	'Were you born in a barn?'
Distancing:	'I don't want to listen to you anymore.'
Using age as a put-down:	'A three-year-old could do this.'

(DfES 2003)

Modelling

A teaching assistant can model appropriate behaviour or point out other students who are setting a good example. Let's go back to the case of Jody. A teaching assistant, in discussing behavioural issues at a later point and in private with Jody, could say that she always treats Jody with respect and expects Jody to treat her with respect. The teaching assistant could also point out other students who are behaving well, perhaps mentioning Amanda as an example. The teaching assistant could say, 'Amanda always listens to the teacher and always works hard in class.'

However, the question is would Jody want to imitate Amanda? Would Jody say, 'Yes, I want to be like Amanda', or would she say 'Amanda! That swot!'. Would Amanda appreciate being used as a role model? This illustrates the difficulty in finding an appropriate role model. An appropriate role model is one that is not only behaving in an appropriate manner as defined by the teacher and the teaching assistant but is also a student who is admired by their peers.

Remove the audience

If you have difficult things to say to an individual, it is always best to have the conversation in private. You could talk to the student after class, or you could have a quiet chat with the student in the corner of the classroom. The reasons behind this are several. If a student finds that arguing with the teaching assistant gains them approval from their peers, it is important to not play their game. As soon as a student becomes argumentative, you could suggest continuing the discussion in private. Also, in a public confrontation with a student there is a danger that the student will feel unable to back down. A private discussion offers the opportunity to listen to what you have to say, without loosing credibility within the peer group.

Tactical ignoring: focus on primary behaviour and ignore secondary behaviour

Rogers (2000) in discussing behaviour management talks about the distinction between primary behaviour and secondary behaviour. Primary behaviour is the inappropriate behaviour that gets the student into trouble in the first place. Secondary behaviour is any other inappropriate behaviour that has occurred in the course of you, the teaching assistant, trying to confront the student's initial inappropriate behaviour. Let's take the following example.

Teaching assistant:	(Notices Rory snatching the ruler from Sam and then hitting Sam over the head with the ruler.) Rory, what are you doing?
Rory:	Miss, it is not my fault. He started it.
Teaching assistant:	Well. It's going to end now. We have a rule in this class regarding how to behave. What do you say to Sam?
Rory:	Miss, you are always picking on me. I'm always getting into trouble. Why doesn't Sam get told off?
Teaching assistant:	(Remaining calm.) What do you say?
Rory:	It's not fair!
Teaching assistant:	(Remaining calm.) Rory? What do you say?
Rory:	Sorry.
Teaching assistant:	Right you two, let's see both of you trying to get some work done.

What this example illustrates is that the teaching assistant remains focused on the primary behaviour (snatching the ruler and hitting another student with the ruler and how this behaviour broke class rules). In this example the teaching assistant tactically ignores the secondary behaviour (complaints regarding whether being told off is fair or not). By focusing on the primary behaviour, repeating your comments calmly in the manner of a broken record, the student soon comes around and apologises for the episode. This strategy can be very useful.

The teaching assistant in this example could have easily responded to the complaints of the student by saying: 'Rory, don't take that tone of voice with me'. But that response could have made the situation worse. What this approach argues is that, sometimes, tactically ignoring minor inappropriate behaviour is actually helpful.

What is difficult with an approach of tactically ignoring behaviour, is to know the limits of what can be ignored and what can't. Imagine if the situation had gone like this:

Teaching assistant:	(Notices Rory snatching the ruler from Sam and hitting Sam over the head with the ruler) Rory, what are you doing?
Rory:	Miss, it is not my fault. He started it.
Teaching assistant:	Well. It's going to end now. We have rules in this class regarding how to behave. What do you say to Sam?
Rory:	Sam's a f****** idiot and I'm not going to apologise!

Although this episode started off the same, this example is more serious in that Rory has used inappropriate language. The question is whether you can ignore this behaviour or not. Knowing your school's behaviour policy will guide you in this regard. The problem with ignoring inappropriate behaviour, is that it can give the wrong message to the student, in this case that swearing is acceptable within the classroom.

Checklist of strategies

✓ Make use of structured observations that identify antecedents, behaviour and consequences. If possible try to identify what triggers the inappropriate behaviour then remove the trigger. Intervene early.
✓ Create learning environments that are productive. Play your role in making sure that tasks set are achievable and sufficiently challenging.
✓ Catch students when they are good.
✓ Reward and praise appropriate behaviour.
✓ Model appropriate behaviour. Point out students who are behaving well so they can act as role models.
✓ Remove the audience.
✓ Tactically ignore minor misbehaviour. Focus on primary behaviour and ignore secondary behaviour if possible.

Behaviour determined by feelings or emotions

Explanations

In the previous section, we talked about how our behaviour could be explained by consequences. However, consequences such as rewards and punishments only tell part of the story. This viewpoint argues that behaviour is determined by emotions and feelings. Therefore, to change behaviour we need to focus on changing emotions and feelings. Much of what we do is influenced by how we feel. However, while behaviour can easily be described in objective terms, describing how someone is feeling is not always so easy. If we are honest about our own feelings, then sometimes we could say that there are times when we are not sure exactly how we are feeling. Sometimes we try to cover up our true feelings. Sometimes we put on a brave face. If this is true for ourselves, then it will be true for the students we are working with. Here we need to use observation skills, noting not only what was said but what was not said, and, importantly, body language in order to come up with our 'best guess' about how someone is feeling. In a sense, we are using our experience of life to read between the lines. In the previous example of Jody we noted her behaviour as detailed below.

Antecedent	Behaviour
The rest of the class have started the maths worksheet and are on question 4. Jody has not begun the worksheet.	Jody is looking at everyone else working.
The teacher calls out, 'Jody! Haven't you started yet? What are you waiting for? Christmas! I don't want any of your nonsense today.'	Jody glares at the teacher.
The TA approaches and asks if she needs any help to get started.	Jody looks up and notices the other students are now all looking at her. Jody pushes her papers off her desk and yells, 'This is a f***** useless class!'

What is described is a fairly objective account of what has happened. But if we were to try to read between the lines how would we describe how Jody was feeling?

- We might guess that Jody was feeling intimidated by the other students who could do the work. Jody might have felt stupid.
- We might guess that Jody felt the teacher was putting her down and that the teaching assistant was just showing her up in front of her peers as someone who was 'thick'.

As stated previously, it is very difficult to know exactly what someone else is feeling. We have to make guesses based on behaviour. We could ask Jody? But would she tell us? Under what circumstances would she tell us? We will come back to this point.

What we are saying is that one response to feeling bad, inadequate, stupid is to lash out and behave inappropriately. When psychologists talk about feelings they talk about concepts such as self-esteem, ideal self, self-image and self-concept. It is important at this point to define these terms.

- *Self-concept* is the whole us. Self-concept is composed of ideal-self, self-image and self-esteem.
- *Self-image* is how we see or describe ourselves to ourselves. Do we see ourselves as clever, beautiful, artistic, thick, thin, clumsy, etc.?
- *Ideal self* is how we would like to be. We might be a brunette, but really we would much prefer to be a blonde. We might be getting 80 per cent in all our tests, but really 80 per cent is not good enough and what we want is 90 per cent.
- *Self-esteem* is how we evaluate ourselves. It is the difference between the way we see ourselves (self-image), and our ideal-self, the way we would like to be.

Whether we have a low or high self-esteem depends on how we evaluate ourselves. Therefore you cannot assume that a student with high ability will necessarily have high self-esteem. As stated earlier a student may be getting 80 per cent in all tests, but that is just not enough. Likewise, a student who is failing all his subjects might have high self-esteem.

Harter (1982) stated that we evaluate ourselves in four areas:

Situation	Response: put-down	Framed positively
Everyone else in the group has finished their work except Sam. It is now break-time.	TA says, 'What do you mean, you haven't finished the work? How much time do you need?'	TA says, 'I see you have worked very hard on this worksheet [praising effort and hopefully boosting self-esteem]. You still need to complete the next three questions [stating a fact]. We will do this next time.'

Corrective feedback should be constructive

It is easy to give feedback to a student when they have done a great job. 'Wow that painting is brilliant!' 'Fabulous!' 'You got all the questions right.' But what do we say when students have not understood? What do you say when they have completely messed up the worksheet? And more importantly how do you say it in a way that will not undermine their sense of self-worth and confidence as a learner? Consider the following example.

Teaching assistant: Sam, let me have a look at your work? (You notice that every answer on the sheet is wrong.)

Sam: Am I right? Do I get a sticker?

Teaching assistant: Sam, I can see that you have tried very hard (praising effort, boosting self-esteem) but I think we need to look at these questions again.

Sam: You mean I am wrong? (Sam seems visibly upset, picks up his textbook and throws it across the room.)

What is interesting about the example is that even though the teaching assistant was very careful not to use the word 'wrong', the student very quickly realised that his answers were wrong. Could the teaching assistant have responded differently? Perhaps more attention should have been paid to the worksheet that he had been given in the first place. As we stated in the previous section, work should not be given to a student if the work is beyond their capabilities.

One rule in giving constructive feedback is that for every one thing that you tell the student that they didn't do, or that they should have done, you need to tell them *four* things that they have done well. Usually you will mention three good points, one point in need of attention and then finish off with another good point. Of course, the praise has to be genuine and has to be seen as such. We will return to our example.

Teaching assistant: Sam, let me have a look at your work? (You notice that every answer on the sheet is wrong.)

Sam: Am I right? Do I get a sticker?

Teaching assistant: Sam, your handwriting has really improved. All the numbers are on the line correctly and written very neatly. Well done! You have worked very hard this session and have not been out of your seat once. (Praising what Sam has done will boost self-esteem.) However, I think we need to look at these questions again.

I know what you have done. You have added the numbers instead of subtracting. If this was an addition question, it would be correct. (Finding a reason for his mistake, but also affirming his understanding of maths, thereby, boosting self-esteem.) Let's have another go at these questions later.

Sam:	Do I get a sticker?
Teaching assistant:	Yes, Sam, you certainly deserve one.

There are times when everyone needs corrective feedback. There is a real art in giving corrective feedback in a constructive manner, that is, in a way that preserves self-worth and encourages the student to keep trying. Of course, the easy way out of the situation would be not to pick up on students' mistakes. Then the student would feel good, they wouldn't get upset or angry, but, of course, they would not be learning.

Making a distinction between the behaviour and the person

When a student misbehaves, it is important to separate the behaviour from the person. Let's return to the example of Sam.

Teaching assistant:	Sam, I can see that you have tried very hard (praising effort, boosting self-esteem) but I think we need to look at these questions again.
Sam:	You mean I am wrong? (Sam seems visibly upset, picks up his textbook and throws it across the room.)

One way of approaching this situation would be to say:

Teaching assistant:	Sam, you are a naughty boy!

Or you could say:

Teaching assistant:	Sam, you know that throwing books is not allowed in the class.

In the second approach the teaching assistant is making a distinction between the student and the behaviour. The behaviour is wrong. The first approach made connections between the behaviour and the person. Because the behaviour was wrong, the person was also wrong and naughty. The difficulty with this approach is that it can lead the student to identify with the label, 'I am naughty'. In a sense this label becomes part of their self-image, their personal description of themselves. If students believe themselves to be naughty then they could act accordingly.

Modelling emotional awareness

In the explanations section we looked at a very impressive definition of emotional intelligence. Teachers and teaching assistants have a role to play in helping the student to recognise and deal with emotions. Teaching assistants can model emotional awareness by talking about their own emotions and how they deal with them.

Consider the following sympathetic interaction.

Jody:	I just can't do maths!
Teaching assistant:	Maths is difficult.
Jody:	When I can't do something, I just want to give up.
Teaching assistant:	It's important to keep trying. When I was learning to drive, I just couldn't get the hang of reversing around the corner. No matter what my driving instructor said, I just couldn't do it. I felt stupid, especially since everyone else seemed to be able to do it so easily. I wanted to just pack it in. But I kept trying and eventually I did it.
	Now, about last session when you swore at me.
Jody:	Miss, I never!

Teaching assistant:	Now, Jody, I imagine that the reason you swore was that you were very upset about the fact that you were finding the maths worksheet difficult.
Jody:	Miss.
Teaching assistant	But Jody, I have feelings and when you swear at me, it makes me feel very upset.
Jody:	Sorry, Miss.

Active listening

Active listening is about effective communication, about demonstrating to the person with whom you are talking with that you have really heard what they have been saying and, importantly, that you understand what they are saying. Active listening is a very useful technique in any work situation but it becomes absolutely essential when you are trying to deal with episodes of inappropriate behaviour, whether you are trying to make a student behave or discussing with a student all the possible reasons for their misbehaviour. Active listening involves many techniques and the application of various skills as outlined below (Nelson-Jones 1993).

Knowing the difference between me and you

It is important to remember that each individual, including yourself, has their own unique perspective of both themselves and of others. For example, you might think that a student has a problem managing their anger, as they are very quick to lash out at any student who has an argument with them. However, the student might consider an aggressive response to be a matter of ensuring respect and credibility and that as a teaching assistant you could not possibly understand. The first step in active listening is to try to get inside the student's mind and see the world from their perspective.

Maintain an attitude of respect and acceptance

This involves accepting that each individual has their own unique thoughts and feelings. Active listening involves listening to what a student says without making judgements. Thus, when the student says that hitting someone is all about 'street cred', to dismiss the idea of 'street cred' as just nonsense would not be respecting or understanding their point of view. Of course, that is not to say that punching someone in order to preserve your 'street cred' is right or acceptable!

Sending good body and voice messages

We can communicate to the student that we are listening through the use of positive body language. This would include having a relaxed posture, facing the student, maintaining eye contact, leaning slightly forward. With a very young child it would be important to get down to their level. It is vital not to get too close; invading an individual's personal space is seen as threatening. Likewise, we need to moderate our tone of voice, so as not to appear frightening or threatening. If a student has lost control, it does not help if the teaching assistant loses control as well. The best approach is to try to remain calm. By remaining calm there is less chance of aggravating the situation. If a student has lost control it is better to position yourself at an angle to the student rather than directly in front of them, as that might seem confrontational. On the other hand, if we want to communicate to the student that we mean what we say, a firm, no-nonsense tone of voice is needed.

Reading others' body language

As we become aware of what our own body language communicates to others, it is also important to start reading what the students are communicating through their body language. As a teaching assistant you spend many hours supporting the same students and over time you begin to pick up on each student's unique body language. Often there are certain non-verbal behaviours that indicate when a person is in the process of losing their temper. These non-verbal behaviours include:

- levels of activity – the student could become restless, leave their seat or become very quiet;
- facial tension and expression;
- eye contact – the eyes could widen or there could be a reluctance to maintain eye contact.

As you gain experience in your role you will begin to pick up on these non-verbal clues and possibly be able to intervene before the situation gets out of hand.

Verbal and non-verbal techniques

These techniques include the use of openers, small rewards, open-ended questions, rewording and reflecting feelings. These techniques would not be effective when a student is in the middle of an outburst. However, it is possible that these techniques could be used as soon as you realise that a student is becoming agitated. Or they can be employed when the dust settles and you have the opportunity to discuss their behaviour with the student.

- *Openers* – These are statements that give the student permission to talk. For example: 'You seem upset . . . are you alright?'
- *Small rewards* – These are non-verbal responses you give to a student to communicate that you are listening. Non-verbal responses include nods, raised eyebrows, good eye contact and soothing voice sounds.
- *Open-ended questions* – Questions such as 'How are you feeling?' encourage the student to keep talking.
- *Rewording* – This involves listening to what a student is saying, re-phrasing what they have said in your mind and then saying this back to the student. This strategy communicates to the student that you are listening, it helps you to understand what the student is saying and it may also help the student to understand what they are saying.
- *Reflecting feelings* – This involves not only listening to what a student is saying, but noting the manner in which they are speaking as this gives clues to how the student is feeling. For example: 'you say you are fine but your hands are shaking'. Sometimes you can also reflect back to the student what you think may be the reasons for their feelings.

At this point let's look at an example. Celia, a teaching assistant in a secondary school comments on Brad.

> Brad is a student whom I support. He has difficulty controlling his temper. I noticed another lad in the class, Bill, pass him and say out loud that there was a terrible smell in the classroom. I could see Brad tense his shoulders. I knew that was not a good sign. I walked quickly over to Brad and asked if I could have a quiet word with him at the back of the classroom.

The first point to notice is that the teaching assistant intervenes early and takes Brad to a place within the class where she can have a private word. At this point the conversation went as follows:

Teaching assistant:	Are you alright, you seem quite tense. (This was an opener.)
Brad:	Miss, it's Bill.
Teaching assistant:	(maintains eye contact, nods) mmmmm. (This is a small reward.)

Teaching assistant:	What did Bill do?
	(This is an open question.)
Brad:	He said there was a bad smell in the classroom.
Teaching assistant:	You are upset because Bill said there was a bad smell in the classroom?
	(Rewording.)
Brad:	I could punch him!
Teaching assistant:	You are feeling angry because Bill said there was a bad smell, perhaps you feel angry because you think he might be making that comment about you?
	(Reflecting feelings and reasons.)
Brad:	Yeah.

The teaching assistant, by acknowledging Brad's emotions, has diffused a potentially difficult situation. Of course, there is the issue of what you should say to Brad, once you have helped him to become aware of his emotions. Brad needs to examine how he thinks about this situation. We will come back to this example in the next section.

Removing the audience

In the previous example the teaching assistant had a conversation regarding a sensitive issue in private. In a private conversation you can talk about more personal issues and feelings. If this conversation were to occur within earshot of the other students, the student in question would be mindful of how what he said could be interpreted. Had the student in this example had an audience, he might have felt the need to punch the other student in order not to lose face. In a sense we are talking about dealing with students in a sensitive manner that preserves their self-esteem.

Checklist of strategies

✓ Support or stigma? Be aware of how students perceive support? If students find it difficult to accept support a gentle approach is needed.
✓ Be aware of all aspects of communication. Use active listening techniques.
✓ Language should be positive.
✓ Corrective feedback should be constructive.
✓ Corrective discipline should make a distinction between the behaviour and the person.
✓ Teaching assistants can model emotional awareness.
✓ Remove the audience. Say important things in private.

Behaviour determined by thoughts or thinking processes

Explanations

This viewpoint argues that behaviour is determined by the way we think. Therefore, to change behaviour we need to focus on changing our thoughts or thinking processes. In this section we will deal with how students think about inappropriate behaviour. Many psychologists talk about how children's thinking changes with time. Of particular interest in this section is the work on moral development, how children learn what is right and what is wrong and how their thinking regarding moral development changes with time.

The first theory we will look at is outlined by Piaget. Piaget (1970) believes that there are three stages of moral development as detailed in Table 2.1.

Table 2.1 Piaget's theory of moral development

Stage	Age	Features
Pre-moral	0–5 years	Children have very little understanding of rules or other aspects of moral development, although children begin to develop this as they near the age of 5.
Moral realism	5–10 years	Children are rigid in their thinking.
		Rules are important and must always be obeyed. For example, it is important to tell the truth ('You smell!') even if it means hurting someone's feelings.
		Consequences are more important than the intentions. If you accidentally break your friend's toy, you are still naughty.
		The naughtier the behaviour, the greater the punishment should be.
		Naughty behaviour will always be punished in some way.
		There is no concept yet that punishment should include some notion of making amends; that is, if you purposely break your friend's toy you should try to fix it or buy them another one.
Moral relativism	Upwards of 10 years	Children can think more flexibly about moral issues.
		They realise that people have different rules about what is right and what is wrong.
		They realise that sometimes it is OK to break a rule. For example, sometimes you need to lie, so as not to hurt someone's feelings.
		When deciding what is wrong, the child now takes into account the intentions of the individual as well as the consequences.
		'Tommy didn't mean to break my car, he just stepped on it, as he didn't see it. Tommy is not naughty it was just an accident!'
		Children believe that the punishment should fit the crime and that the guilty party should try to make amends.
		Children are aware that sometimes people who misbehave do get away with it.

Source: (Eysenck and Flanagan 2001)

Kohlberg (1981) outlined another theory of moral development as detailed in Table 2.2. Kohlberg believed, as did Piaget that moral reasoning developed with time. Research evidence indicates that in children between the ages of 10 and 16 there is an increase in moral reasoning at level 2, conventional morality (Eysenck and Flanagan 2001). Although somewhat complex, these theories on moral development are important to be aware of. We will come to the reasons why this is so shortly.

The next research to be outlined involves the relationship between parental styles of discipline and moral development. Although this talks about the actions of parents, this can be applied to the classroom.

Table 2.2 Kohlberg's theory of moral development

Level 1   *Pre-conventional morality* – At this level what is considered right or wrong is determined by whether you are punished or rewarded. Thus, pushing in line is *wrong* because you will be told off, or, helping the teacher is *right*, as getting a sticker will reward you.

Level 2   *Conventional morality* – In this stage individuals behave either out of a desire to win approval from others or out of a fear that others will somehow blame them if they misbehave. At this stage it is not only the consequences of your behaviour that are important but the social aspects – that is, what others think of you. At the end of this stage individuals believe that it is one's duty to obey the laws and rules of society.

Level 3   *Post-conventional morality* – This is the highest level of moral development. Here, the individual develops more abstract notions of justice and morality. Here, individuals can appreciate the difference between the letter and the spirit of the law.

Research (Hoffman 1982) has revealed that there are three styles used in trying to encourage moral development as detailed below.

- *Power assertion* – includes physical punishment, spankings, harsh words, removal of privileges.
- *Love withdrawal* – this involves withdrawing attention and affection from the child if they misbehave: 'I won't like you if you do that'.
- *Induction* – this involves reasoning and explaining why a certain action is wrong, specifically stressing the effect that the behaviour has on other people.

Brody and Shaffer (1982) reviewed many studies relating parenting styles to the child's moral development. Their findings are given below.

- *Induction* (reasoning) improved moral development in 86 per cent of studies.
- *Love withdrawal* (withdrawing affection and attention) improved moral development in 42 per cent of studies.
- *Power assertion* (harsh words, removal of privileges) improved moral development in 18 per cent of studies. However, it was also found that *power assertion* had a negative effect on moral development in 82 per cent of studies. Zahn-Waxler *et al.* (1979) found that *power assertion* results in children who are aggressive and do not care about others. Possibly this is true because the child is learning to imitate the aggressive techniques that are used on them.

This research has important implications for teaching assistants, as the lesson to be learnt is that the way to encourage appropriate behaviour is to use reasoning. The theories of moral development, although complex, can give a broad idea of how an individual child is thinking about what is right and wrong. In a sense you start with the level of reasoning that a child has reached and then try to move them forward. So for children at Piaget's stage of moral realism (5–10 years) or Kohlberg's pre-conventional morality you will need to talk about rules, the consequences of rules and the difference between consequences and intentions.

A more recent development in this area concerns cognitive behavioural therapy (CBT). Maladaptive behaviour, in this case inappropriate behaviour in the classroom, is due to irrational or faulty thinking. This approach acknowledges that emotions and thoughts are interconnected. Perhaps one reason for inappropriate behaviour is that the student does not think, but simply reacts. Instead of thinking for the student, a teacher or teaching assistant needs to develop an awareness of the student's own thinking processes. A way forward (Gourley 1999, Hymans 2003, De Bono 1999) is to help students to broaden the way they look at situations, to encourage students to look at situations from different perspectives and to help them realise that there are different ways of responding to situations. This brings us to the next section on strategies.

Strategies

Corrective language

In simple terms corrective language relates to how we tell a student off for misbehaving. There are many ways to tell a student off, but what we are interested in are methods that will:

- preserve self-esteem;
- encourage and develop reasoning and thinking skills;
- lead to the student behaving appropriately in the future.

A number of techniques that can be employed are discussed below.

Does the student know what they are supposed to be doing?

When a student displays inappropriate behaviour you need to ask yourself why they are behaving in this way. Do they know what to do? Have they forgotten what to do? Do they just need to be reminded? The four versions outlined below offer some alternative responses to the scenario of the teaching assistant observing Amanda throwing her apron on the floor, dumping her paint tray and brush in the sink and hurrying off to break.

VERSION 1

Teaching assistant: Amanda. Were you born in a barn?

This comment, although reflecting the teaching assistant's exasperation with Amanda's messy ways, might not prove to be effective. This remark does not tell Amanda what she has done wrong, nor what she should do. The remark is also phrased as a put-down. Amanda could easily think that the teaching assistant is just having a go at her. There is also the issue of whether Amanda would understand the teaching assistant's remark.

VERSION 2

Teaching assistant: Amanda we have a rule in this class for cleaning up our equipment. Thank you.

In this example the teaching assistant reminds the student of the rule. Hopefully by focusing on the rule, the reminder is not seen as a personal put-down. By saying 'thank you', the teaching assistant is communicating to Amanda that she believes that she will tidy up. However, this example does not specifically state what Amanda should do or why she should behave in such a way.

VERSION 3

Teaching assistant: Amanda we have a rule in this class for cleaning up our equipment. Paint pots and brushes should be washed out, dried and put away. Aprons should be hung up. When equipment is put away properly it means that it will be ready for the next person to use. You wouldn't want to use a paintbrush that was all dried up with paint and you wouldn't want to put on an apron that was dirty. Thank you, Amanda.

This version again focuses on the rules, but it goes beyond them and states the reasons behind the rules and the personal consequences for others of not following the rules. This will help Amanda to develop more complex ways of reasoning. However, perhaps here the teaching assistant is doing too much of the thinking for Amanda. Perhaps Amanda needs to be encouraged to think for herself.

VERSION 4

Teaching assistant:	Amanda we have a rule in this class for cleaning up our equipment. Paint pots and brushes should be washed out, dried and put away. Aprons should be hung up.
	Amanda, what happens if we don't clean the paint brushes and we don't hang the aprons up?
Amanda:	I wouldn't like to wear an apron if someone stepped all over it?
Teaching assistant:	That's right, Amanda! When equipment is put away properly it means that it will be ready for the next person to use. Thank you, Amanda.

Double questions

When you notice that someone is not doing what he or she should be doing it is useful to ask the student:

- what are you doing?
- what should you be doing?

These questions encourage the students to think about what they are doing as shown in the following exchange.

Teaching assistant:	(Notices two students looking at a magazine rather than completing their worksheet.) Girls, what are you doing?
Amy:	Magazine, miss?
Teaching assistant:	What should you be doing?
Amy:	Doing the worksheet.
Teaching assistant:	Yes, I will come and have a look at your work in a minute.

When – then

In a sense this can be seen as a type of agreement between you and the student. You are stating what they have to do before they get to do what they want. Again, this involves reasoning.

Teaching assistant:	When you have cleaned up the paint equipment, then you can go out for break.

Partial agreement

This technique can be useful when you are in a situation where you are asking a student to do something and they are trying to argue why they shouldn't have to do what you say. This situation is particularly common in secondary schools and in part is due to older students' ability to reason. Let's return to the example of the girls and the magazine.

Teaching assistant:	Girls, what are you doing?
Amy:	Magazine, miss?
Teaching assistant:	What should you be doing?
Amy:	Miss Todd, who was with us last week, let us have our magazine out? She said we could have our magazine on the desk.

| Teaching assistant: | Well, maybe Miss Todd did say you could have your magazine out (partial agreement) but I am asking you to put it away and get on with your work. |

Making students aware of the impact of their behaviour on others

In this technique you give feedback or tell the student what they are doing, the effect this has on others and how this behaviour makes you feel. Again, what you are trying to do is to make students more aware of the reasons for rules and the consequences that breaking the rules has for others.

Teaching assistant:	Tom, can you please stop making frog noises. Thank you.
Tom:	(Still keeps making noises.)
Teaching assistant:	Tom, making those noises is going against one of our classroom rules. When you make those noises, I can't hear myself think and I certainly can't hear what the others in the group are saying. That means I can't help them get on with the questions on the worksheet. I don't know how they are feeling, but that noise gives me a headache and makes me feel angry.
Tom:	Sorry, Miss.

Time to respond

Sometimes it is helpful, after asking a student to do something or not to do something, to give them time to respond. Again, let's look at the example of the girls and the magazine.

Teaching assistant:	Girls, what are you doing?
Amy:	Magazine, miss?
Teaching assistant:	Put it away.
Girls:	(Look defiant and start flipping through magazine.)
Teaching assistant:	(Towering over the girls and raising voice) I said put it away now!

In this example what the teaching assistant has done is to back the students into a corner and provoked a confrontation. Hopefully, the girls will put the magazine away, but what will the teaching assistant do if they don't? In this example the teaching assistant's approach has possibly made the situation worse. This situation could have been avoided if the teaching assistant had taken a slightly different approach. Rogers (2000) refers to this as the least to most intrusive approach. Rogers (2000) argues that it is best to intervene in the least intrusive manner possible and move on to a more direct manner, or more forceful approach if, and only if, required. The least intrusive or a more softly-softly approach would go like this.

Teaching assistant:	Girls, what are you doing?
Amy:	Magazine, miss?
Teaching assistant:	Can you put the magazine away and get on with your work. I will come and check in a few minutes.

In this example the teaching assistant communicated to the students what they should be doing and, importantly, gave them time to think about it and time to respond. This prevented a confrontation. However, if the girls refuse to put away the magazine and are still looking at it when the teaching assistant goes back to check then a more direct approach is needed. Usually at that point a discussion regarding choices and consequences would be appropriate.

Language of choice

This is a more direct approach that is used when the student clearly does not want to do what you have asked them. Again, this approach focuses on encouraging the student to actively think about what they are doing and what they are going to do next. Here, you are helping the student to look at the possible consequences of their actions and to make a choice about how they are going to behave. Let's look at the example of Brad, where Brad was angry when Bill made a comment regarding a bad smell in the classroom. The teaching assistant is having a quiet word with Brad.

Brad:	I could punch him!
Teaching assistant:	Well Brad, you could punch him, but what would happen if you did?
Brad:	I would feel better?
Teaching assistant:	What else would happen?
Brad:	I would get a detention.
Teaching assistant:	Yeah, you would get punished. You have a choice about what to do. I don't know what Bill meant when he made that remark, but I know that you have been behaving well in class and it would be a shame to spoil that. Again, you have the choice. You could punch him and get into trouble or you could sit down and carry on with your work.

Brad listened to what the teaching assistant said, went back to his seat and carried on with his work. At the end of the lesson the teaching assistant gave him a commendation note for his behaviour in class.

In this example a discussion about the consequences of actions and stressing that the student has a choice encouraged the student to think about their actions and, in the end, behave appropriately.

Emphasise the relationship between behaviour and outcomes

This strategy involves what happens when the student does not make good choices, for example in the previous scenario, if Brad went back to class, walked up to Bill and punched him. This strategy involves trying to get the student to think about their behaviour, why they did what they did and how they are going to make amends. Again, the emphasis is on trying to get the student to think about their behaviour.

Rogers (2000: 38) recommends that the student thinks about the following.

- What did I do?
- Why do I think this happened?
- What rule did I break?
- What do I need to do to fix things up?

Encouraging this line of reasoning helps the student to repair and rebuild relationships. This is essential because at the end of the day the students will still be in the same class and you, the teaching assistant, will still be working with those same students.

Involve the students in rule making

This technique can be particularly useful when working with small groups. Instead of waiting for the group to start to play up, you give them clear guidance and reminders of how you expect them to behave. For example, 'In this group, we have a rule regarding speaking – when we want to speak we put our hands up' or 'In this group, we have rules about how to listen'. Sometimes it is very useful to have the group discuss and decide on group rules among themselves. In this case the advice is that:

- you clarify or explain to the students the need for the rules;
- that you have as few rules as possible;
- that the rules are written in a positive manner, i.e. 'We will listen to what each other has to say', rather than, 'We will not interrupt'.

Table 2.3 Special needs

Difficulties in:	Conditions where these difficulties might occur	Impact on behaviour	Ways in which a teaching assistant can help
Coordination These students might appear clumsy. They could have problems with fine motor skills (handwriting, tying their shoelaces, getting dressed after PE) or gross motor skills (jumping, running, kicking a ball).	Dyspraxia, Down's syndrome	• Frustration can easily develop as the student struggles to do tasks which most students find easy. • The student might be teased by other students or not included in games or activities. • Isolation and frustration can lead to low self-esteem and incidents where the student lashes out at others.	Praise the student often to raise self-esteem. Be aware of the student's limitations and do not put the student into situations or give them tasks that they can't do. As far as possible try to make life more manageable, for example allow them extra time to get changed for PE.
Limited auditory short-term memory These students will have difficulties in remembering instructions and directions. If the teacher asks the students to take their textbooks to the back of the class, put their work on her desk and then go and stand by the door, a student with difficulties in this area might get to the back of the class and forget why they are there.	Dyslexia Dyspraxia Down's syndrome	• This student might appear not to be doing what they should be doing but this is not because they are being disobedient, it is simply because they have not understood the instructions. • The student may not have completed their homework because they simply forgot.	Be on hand to remind the student of instructions. Encourage the student to ask others or yourself if they are not certain. Do not give complex instructions. Ensure that the homework that is set is written correctly in the planner.
Lack of organisational skills Here the student has difficulty in remembering what to bring to school, what they need for each lesson and where they should be at a certain time.	Dyspraxia Dyslexia Attention deficit hyperactivity disorder (ADHD)	• A student who consistently forgets to bring the proper equipment to class and who forgets where they should be will be told off.	A teaching assistant can provide reminders to the student. It has on occasion been known for a teaching assistant, especially in a large secondary school, to meet a student at the beginning of the day to check that they have all their equipment and that they know what they should be doing.
Social skills: understanding others This child will have difficulties in maintaining friendships. They will often lack empathy. They will find it difficult to understand others' verbal and non-verbal behaviour. They will not be good at reading facial expressions or understanding emotions.	Autistic spectrum disorder (ASD)	• Such individuals can annoy their peers without realising. For example, a 14-year-old lad with ASD goes up to a large sixth former and comments in a loud voice: 'Your spots are enormous. Do you squeeze them?' The 14-year-old with ASD is surprised when the sixth former then punches him.	The teaching assistant, together with the teacher and the SENCO, will implement specialised training packages.

Obsession with routines	Autistic spectrum disorder (ASD)	• An individual with an obsession with routines can become extremely upset and angry when things do not happen as they should. For example, imagine break-time is at 10:30 and the assembly is running over time because Reverend Smith still has a few things to say. Laura, who has ASD, gets up from her seat and announces to Reverend Smith that it is 10:30 and it is break-time. Sally, who is sitting beside Laura, tells her to sit down. At this point Laura starts to scream that it is 10:30, and now it is 10:31!	Again, the teaching assistant, with the teacher and the Senco, will implement specialised interventions such as social stories.
Inattention	Attention deficit hyperactivity disorder (ADHD)	• A student who is inattentive will have difficulty staying on task and is easily distracted. Such a student can be told off many times a day for not doing what they should be doing.	This student will need constant reminders of what they should be doing. This student will benefit from structure and routine and will not easily cope in a class where there are many distractions.
Hyperactivity	Attention deficit hyperactivity disorder (ADHD)	• In this case a student will not be able to keep still. They will be out of their seat more often than they are in it. This student is constantly fidgeting. Obviously this student could be told off many times in the school day.	Such a student will benefit from a very structured classroom environment, where everyone has their own desk and very clear rules regarding appropriate behaviour are firmly in place.
Impulsiveness	Attention deficit hyperactivity disorder (ADHD) Autistic spectrum disorder (ASD)	• This student will blurt out answers before the teacher asks them, will have difficulty waiting their turn and often acts without thinking. These behaviours can lead to the student being told off by the teacher or their peers.	Encourage thinking skills and self-control.

Checklist of strategies

✓ Encourage appropriate behaviour by encouraging reasoning.

✓ When using corrective language it is helpful to ask yourself the following: Does the student know what they are supposed to be doing?

✓ Using double questions – 'What are you doing?', 'What should you be doing?' encourages students to think about their actions.

✓ Partial agreement and the use of when–then statements can be useful.

✓ Making the student aware of the impact of their behaviour on others helps them to become more aware of the reasons for rules and the consequences that breaking rules has on others.

✓ Giving a student time to respond to a request allows time for thinking and avoids unnecessary confrontation.

✓ Using the language of choice helps the student to look at the possible consequences of their actions and to think before acting.

✓ Involving the student in rule making encourages thinking skills.

Special needs

One consideration that we have not looked at is the issue of special needs. Sometimes students with a specific statement of special needs will have particular difficulties with behaviour that you will need to be aware of. When dealing with a student with specific special needs, a teaching assistant will need clear advice and guidance from the teacher and SENCO. Table 2.3 looks at some of these issues. A more detailed discussion of special needs can be found in *A Teaching Assistant's Guide to Child Development and Psychology in the Classroom* by Susan Bentham, published by Routledge.

Summary

In this chapter we have looked at many explanations for inappropriate behaviour and we have also looked at a number of strategies that can be helpful. These explanations and strategies have been discussed in separate sections dealing respectively with:

- behaviour being determined by consequences;
- behaviour being determined by feelings or emotions;
- behaviour being determined by thoughts or thinking processes.

Such a distinction has proved useful in presenting relevant information. However, the reality is that in a classroom situation when a student is not doing what they should be doing, that student's behaviour will be determined by a combination of consequences, feelings and thoughts. In addition, there could be special educational needs or difficulties contributing to their behaviour.

In the reality of the classroom there are no easy answers. Theories and strategies are useful to be aware of as they can help you in dealing with students on a day-to-day basis. Which strategy or combination of strategies works with which student is for you to discover. One method of helping you to discover which approach works best is that of reflection. The rest of the book will focus on common difficulties and will use reflection as a method of trying to discover a way forward.

Chapter 3

The student who is never in their seat

Students refusing to remain seated pose a common problem for teaching assistants. What do you do with the student who finds it difficult to remain in their seat? This might not seem to be a very serious problem, but having to give persistent reminders to a student to stay in their seat reduces the time you have to support other students. Two case studies describing such situations follow.

Primary school

The event

Sarah who works supporting a Year 1 class outlines the first scenario.

> I was working with the Yellow Group. Yellow Group had all drawn a picture of their trip to the local park. The teacher had explained to me that I was to encourage the group to take turns talking about their pictures, asking them why they had chosen to draw what they did.
>
> To begin with I quickly reminded them of the rules of working together – that we must listen to each other. It all went well for the first few minutes. Everyone, including Matthew, was sitting up straight and paying attention. I first talked to Chloe. Chloe had drawn a lovely picture of a pond with ducks and was telling the group how much she liked ducks. It was at this point that I noticed that Matthew was under the table. I asked Matthew what he was up to and did he think he could listen to what was going on when he was under the table. Matthew said he was looking for his pencil that he had dropped but now he had found it. Once Matthew was sitting up at the table, I smiled at him and reminded him of the group rules.
>
> Next it was James's turn to talk about his picture of a train. There is a small train that runs through the park. James said he likes trains and that the train reminded him of 'Thomas the Train'. I then noticed that Matthew was not at the table but over at the other side of the room. I left the group to go and collect Matthew and asked him what he was doing. He just grinned and said that he needed to get something in his drawer. I told Matthew that he knew it was a rule that he should ask permission to leave the group. Matthew said that he did know and that he would behave, and with that I escorted him back to the group.
>
> Next it was Amanda's turn to talk about her drawing of the flowers that she had seen in the park. I commented that Amanda must really like flowers. Amanda said that she did and that she helped her mother in the garden. Well, would you know it, I turned around and Matthew had gone off again. I left the group and again asked him what he was playing at. Matthew said that he had to ask his friend about a birthday party they were to go to after school. I again reminded him of the rules and he said: 'Sorry, I keep forgetting'.
>
> When we got back to the group, Amanda commented that Matthew must have ants in his pants. All the children laughed and Matthew made a show of wriggling around and

scratching his bottom. The children laughed even more. At that point it was time to go out to break.

I commented to the teacher that Matthew was out of his seat more than he was in it. In a space of ten minutes, he had been under the desk once and over at the other side of the room twice.

On reflection

Why do I think Matthew is behaving in such a way?

Matthew is just not very good at listening or taking turns. Matthew has a real problem staying in his seat, although when he is really interested in a subject there is no problem with him being out of his seat.

What strategies did I use?

I followed the correct procedures. At the start of the session I reminded the group of the rules regarding listening and I reminded Matthew of the rules several times during the lesson. I feel I remained calm with Matthew for most of the time.

What worked? What didn't work?

Reminding Matthew of the rules seemed to work in the short term, however, he just did not seem to be able to remember them.

How can I improve my practice?

I am always having problems with Matthew; I feel that there is something that I am missing. Perhaps I am not firm enough?

Secondary school

The event

Jill works in a secondary school supporting students in Year 9. She listened to what Sarah had said and remarked that she supported a student just like Matthew.

Let me tell you about yesterday with Jason. We were in a Year 9 maths class and we were to divide into groups and start completing the exercises from the maths book on rotation. I was in a group with Jason, Mark, Marie and Vicki. I first made sure that all the students had their work books, textbook and pens. While I was flipping through Vicki's textbook to find the right page, I noticed Jason over by the window. I happened to catch his eye and he quickly returned to his seat. He just remarked that it was miserable weather and that he hoped I didn't have my laundry on the line. I told him that we were not in class to talk about my laundry but to do the work assigned on rotation.

All the students had managed to find the right page and we were looking at one of the examples. I was explaining to Marie about rotation, when I noticed that Jason had darted to the back of the class. I again gave him the look and he quickly returned with a set of sharpened pencils. He stated that he thought everyone would appreciate these. Marie remarked about how thoughtful Jason was. Jason is a very popular young man. I thanked Jason for the pencils, but said to the group that we must really get down to work.

We started the next question and I was just explaining a point to Marie when I noticed Jason at the other end of the room. I went over to Jason and asked him what he was doing.

He said that Carla had her hand up to ask a question and as the teacher and I were busy, he went over to see if he could help her. Carla just happens to be his girlfriend. I took Jason over to a quiet corner and said that all this being out of his seat meant that I couldn't spend as much time helping the others and that this made me feel upset and that I felt this wasn't fair on the others. Jason apologised and came back to the group. We only had five minutes left. Jason did remain in his seat, however he did very little work.

On reflection

Why do I think Jason is behaving in such a way?

I think that basically Jason is a born charmer and that he just craves attention.

What strategies did I use?

I used 'the look' to bring him back on task. I reminded him of what he should be doing and I had a quiet word with him about how his actions were affecting the others.

What worked? What didn't work?

Giving him 'the look' worked in the short term, but it was only when I had a quiet word with him that he finally remained in his seat?

How can I improve my practice?

You can't help liking Jason, however his out-of-seat, all-over-the room behaviour does wind me up. Although eventually he settled, I wasted valuable time getting him to stay in his seat. Perhaps I should have had a quiet talk about his behaviour earlier in the session.

Self-assessment questions

- What do you think are the possible explanations for Matthew and Jason's out-of-seat behaviour?
- What specific strategies do you think the teaching assistants used?
- What would you do if you were the teaching assistant?

Making sense of behaviour

Both of the above case studies describe students, though of varying ages, who have the same difficulty in remaining in their seats. Although we only have limited information, we can attempt to make educated guesses (based on what we have discussed about behaviour) regarding why they are doing what they are doing. Hopefully the various explanations will suggest strategies that will help them to remain in their seats. The rest of this chapter will look in turn at the three views (behaviour determined by consequences, behaviour determined by emotions and feelings, and behaviour determined by thoughts and thinking processes) in regard to both explanations and ways forward – that is, practical everyday strategies that a teaching assistant can use.

Behaviour determined by consequences

Explanations

Here we remember that behaviour is determined by the consequences of the behaviour. One of the first suggestions from this viewpoint is to carry out a structured observation focusing on antecedents, behaviour and consequences.

From what we have read we could write the following analyses of Matthew's and Jason's behaviour.

Matthew		
Antecedent	Behaviour	Consequence
TA speaking to group regarding rules of working together.	Matthew sitting quietly.	
TA talking to Chloe about her drawing of pond.	Matthew under the table.	TA stops talking to Chloe. TA asks Matthew what he is doing under the table.
	Matthew explains that he was looking for his pencil and that he had found it.	TA smiles at Matthew and reminds him of group rules.
TA talking to James about his picture.	Matthew over at other end of the room.	TA leaves group, finds Matthew and asks him what he is doing.
	Matthew grins and says he needed to get something from his drawer.	TA reminds Matthew that he needed to ask permission to leave the group.
	Matthew says 'yes' and that he will behave.	TA escorts Matthew back to the group.
TA talking to Amanda about her picture.	Matthew goes off to talk to friend.	TA leaves group. TA asks Matthew what is he playing at and reminds Matthew of rules.
	Matthew says 'Sorry', I keep forgetting'.	TA escorts Matthew back.
Amanda says Matthew has got ants in his pants.	Matthew and children in the group laugh. Matthew wriggles and scratches his bottom.	Children laugh even more.

This viewpoint argues that if behaviour is ongoing, as in the case of Matthew leaving his seat, then there must be some sort of reward or pay-off for the student. What then is Matthew's reward for leaving his seat? There are several possibilities.

Attention

The teaching assistant only paid attention to Matthew when he was out of his seat. In fact the times when Matthew left his seat corresponded to the times when the teaching assistant was talking to someone else. The teaching assistant was very gentle in reminding Matthew of the rules. Perhaps Matthew liked the teaching assistant coming to collect him and did not see her gentle reminders as being told off.

Avoidance

Perhaps Matthew is unable or unwilling to participate in the group activity. Perhaps Matthew is bored with the activity?

Approval and attention from peers

Matthew received much attention and laughter when Amanda said he had ants in his pants.

Jason		
Antecedent	Behaviour	Consequence
TA busy making sure all students had books. Working with Vicki flipping through textbook.	Jason at window.	TA happens to catch his eye and gives him 'the look'.
Jason back in seat. Group working on maths problem.	Jason remarks that it was miserable weather and he hopes that the TA hasn't got her laundry on the line.	TA tells him that they are not in class to talk about laundry but to do work.
TA explaining to Marie about rotation.	Jason at back of the class. Jason back with group bringing a set of sharpened pencils. Jason remarks, 'I thought everyone would appreciate these'.	TA gave him the 'look'. Marie comments on how thoughtful Jason was. The TA thanks Jason but reminds him that the group must get down to work.
TA explaining a point to Marie. Carla has her hand up.	Jason at other end of room talking to Carla. Jason states that he was helping Carla as she had her hand up but both TA and the teacher were busy. Jason apologises. Goes back to group. Remains in seat but does very little work.	TA leaves group to collect Jason. Asks Jason what he was doing? Takes Jason over to a quiet corner and tells him the consequences of his behaviour for the others, that is, that 'I (TA) couldn't spend as much time helping the others and this made me feel upset'.

Again, this viewpoint argues that if behaviour is ongoing, as is the case of Jason leaving his seat, then there must be some sort of reward or pay-off for the student. What then is rewarding Jason for leaving his seat? Again, there are several possibilities.

Attention

In this scenario as in the case of Matthew, the teaching assistant paid attention to Jason when he was out of his seat. Jason left his seat when the teaching assistant was paying attention to someone else. Although the teaching assistant gave Jason 'the look' for being out of his seat, she thanked him for returning with a set of sharpened pencils.

Avoidance

Perhaps Jason is unable or unwilling to participate. There does seem to be some indication that Jason could be finding the work difficult as even when he does remain in his seat, he does not do much work.

Approval and attention from peers

Jason received positive feedback from the others for bringing them a set of sharpened pencils. Presumably, Jason received pleasurable attention from talking to his girlfriend. What these two examples show is that even though these boys are displaying the same inappropriate behaviour, the reasons for their behaviour could be very different. Of course, as the teaching assistant involved with these two boys you would be in a much better position to determine what is specifically rewarding the behaviour. These observations of student behaviour are important and need to be discussed with the classroom teacher.

Strategies

Try to discover what is triggering the inappropriate behaviour, then remove the trigger

This involves some educated guesswork and entails looking for patterns in the structured observation. If Jason's or Matthew's out-of-seat behaviour is being caused by avoiding a task that they cannot do, or being bored with a task that is not sufficiently challenging, then the teaching assistant needs to discuss with the teacher more appropriate work. It is important that students are given work that they can succeed at. If both Jason's and Matthew's behaviour is being rewarded by the attention they receive then this leads us on to the strategy of rewarding and praising appropriate behaviour.

Rewarding and praising appropriate behaviour

In this instance this means praising Jason and Matthew for remaining in their seats. As Jason is in Year 1, stickers could be given. Perhaps the teacher will organise a reward chart, where for each session during which he remains seated he earns a gold star. A certain number of gold stars can then earn him 15 minutes on a favourite activity of his choice. Certainly, there are rewards and commendations for students in secondary school.

Intervene early

This strategy would involve the teaching assistant picking up on the fact that students were getting restless and at that point involving them positively in the group activity. If the students then participate positively in the group activity then the student can receive praise for appropriate behaviour.

For example, Matthew's teaching assistant could ask all the students to think of a question that they could ask the student who was showing the picture. She could involve Matthew by asking him to question the student about the picture. She could then thank Matthew for his contribution. Jason's teaching assistant could involve Jason by asking him to work with another student and then praise Jason and the other student for working together (assuming that they work together in a positive manner). A more straightforward approach would have the teaching assistant sitting close by the pupil, so that the teaching assistant would immediately know if the student were about to wander off. An issue in both of these case studies involves when to become firm, when to show the students that you mean what you say.

Point out role models

In the early years it is possible to point out to students those other students who are brilliant at sitting in their seats and doing the work. More care needs to be taken with this approach at secondary school.

Behaviour determined by feelings or emotions

Explanations

As stated previously, negative feelings, such as a fear of failure, are seen as threats to our self-esteem. Ways of dealing with threats to our self-esteem include becoming upset, angry or avoiding the situation. Does this possible explanation fit the examples of Jason and Matthew? Possibly, one of the reasons for Jason's out-of-seat behaviour could be his reluctance to do maths?

Strategies

Assistance can be seen as valued support or as a source of shame

If a student's out-of-seat behaviour is due to avoiding a task that they cannot do then they will need additional support to succeed. The difficulty is knowing how to support a student in a manner that maintains and boosts their self-esteem. Some students will be only too willing to ask for and accept help. Some students will not like to ask, will not like to be helped and will not want to do different work from their peers. The first step is to be aware of the student's reaction and to discuss their reaction with the classroom teacher.

Some students will benefit from working in a group who are at the same level. Sometimes students will appreciate working in a different environment on a catch-up session away from their peers. In the case study involving Jason, perhaps the out-of-seat behaviour could have been avoided if the teaching assistant had sat down with Jason and gone over the rotation question with him to determine what he could do?

Teaching assistants can model emotional awareness by talking about their emotions and how they deal with them

The role of a teaching assistant is to help students to deal with situations which they find difficult. A teaching assistant can talk about how they feel when they find a task difficult. Such a discussion might help with Jason if difficulty with maths is the reason for his out-of-seat behaviour. This discussion will need to be handled sensitively.

Behaviour determined by thoughts or thinking processes

Explanations

This viewpoint states that what we do can be explained by our thinking processes. In both case studies the teaching assistant spent considerable time reminding the student of the rules. In the example of Matthew, the teaching assistant reminded the group of the rules at the beginning of the session and reminded Matthew every time she had to bring him back to the group. Matthew always promised to behave but at the end admitted to the fact that he kept forgetting. In this case study there was no mention of reasoning with Matthew regarding why rules were important, however this strategy was used with some effect with Jason.

Strategies

Using double questions, 'What are you doing', 'What should you be doing?' encourages the student to think about their actions

The teaching assistant asked Matthew what he was doing under the table and what he was doing when he was over at the other side of the room. The teaching assistant asked Jason what he was doing talking to Carla. Both teaching assistants received explanations but perhaps they needed to ask the students what they *should be doing*, this would have encouraged the students to think about the rules for themselves.

Making the student aware of the impact of their behaviour on others helps them to become more aware of the reasons for rules

In the case study involving Jason, the teaching assistant used this strategy effectively. However, although it had the result of keeping Jason in his seat, he did not do very much work. This could indicate that there are other reasons why he is getting up from his seat. Although reasoning might work on a short-term basis, unless the root cause of his out-of-seat behaviour is found, the behaviour could continue.

Would this style of reasoning work with Matthew? It would be useful to try this approach. Matthew did say that he knew the rules but that he kept forgetting. Perhaps what Matthew needs is some visual reminder? Suppose Matthew loved trains, then perhaps he could wear a badge that reads: 'Thomas says "Stay in your seat"'.

Giving the student a choice and stating the consequences

For both students perhaps the teaching assistants could have intervened earlier and said firmly that they had a choice to remain in their seat and do their work or have their behaviour reported to the teacher.

Self-assessment questions

- After reading the suggestions in this chapter, how would you have dealt with the students who were never in their seats?
- Think of a situation where you have had to deal with a student's out-of-seat behaviour. Use the techniques in this chapter to think of both explanations for the behaviour and strategies that could turn the behaviour around?

Summary

This chapter has discussed possible explanations and strategies for dealing with students who are never in their seats. In doing this we have looked specifically at two case studies. What we have discovered through this discussion is that there are a number of possible explanations for the behaviour as well as a number of possible strategies that can be used to deal with it. Which strategy, or combination of strategies, you should use in the classroom very much depends on the individual student and the particular details of the situation.

Remember

✓ Write down notes of what happened.
✓ Reflect on what has happened. Ask yourself:

- Why do I think this student is behaving in such a way?
- What strategies did I use?
- What worked? What didn't work?
- How can I improve my practice?

✓ Try to record your recollection of the events in the form of a structured observation noting the antecedents, behaviour and consequences.
✓ Discuss your thoughts with others (teachers, SENCO, other teaching assistants).
✓ Look for possible explanations for behaviour. Consider the consequences, feelings and emotions, and thinking processes as being part of the explanation as well as suggesting ways forward.

Chapter 4

The student who disrupts other students

Dealing with students who disrupt other students is an ongoing task for most teaching assistants. Ideally, the teaching assistant is looking for long-term as well as short-term solutions. What follows are two case studies that describe students who continually disrupt others.

Primary school

Background

Ryan works in a primary school as a teaching assistant. Much of Ryan's time is spent supporting John. John is in Year 3. John has difficulties getting on with the other students in his class. Most of them see him as annoying at best. Although John does seem to have a following among some of the boys in the years below, Ryan states that John sees himself as being tough, a 'bit of a lad'.

The event

Ryan describes what happened on one Monday morning.

> It started during carpet time. The teacher was reading a story to the class. John was sitting behind Dana. Dana has very long blonde hair, which she wears in braids. While the teacher was reading the story, John very gently started to play with Dana's hair. Dana turned around and told him to 'piss off'. The teacher reminded Dana and John to listen. John just looked all innocent. Dana turned back around to the front. At that point, I gave John one of my 'looks'. John seemed to behave himself for a while and then he started again. I think John was trying to tie Dana's braids in a knot. Dana turned around and pushed John over. The teacher at this point intervened and asked both Dana and John to sit at the back of the class as they could not sit still on the carpet. Dana started to protest that John had started it, but John just smirked.
>
> When the time came to do group work. John was sitting beside Kevin and Luke. All the boys seemed to be getting on with their writing. Kevin was working extremely hard. Kevin has difficulty with writing and really has to concentrate on his letter formation. I was at the end of the table helping Luke when I noticed John watching Kevin. Then, John picked up his maths textbook and dropped it inches away from where Kevin was working. Kevin jumped and accidentally scribbled all over his page. Kevin was naturally very upset and yelled: 'Look at what you made me do'. John replied: 'Oh, does a little noise scare little Kevin?'
>
> I called John over and asked him if he thought that was a nice thing to do. He replied that it was just an accident and that he had no way of knowing that Kevin would be so scared and that he shouldn't have to say sorry as it wasn't his fault anyway. I am not sure whether I believed him or not but I decided to give him the benefit of the doubt and said that even

if it was an accident he still should apologise. He turned to Kevin and said: 'Sorry for scaring you Kevi-poo'.

I mentioned all of this to the teacher at break. She stated that disrupting other students was beginning to be a habit with John.

On reflection

Why do I think John is behaving in such a way?

I am not sure. Perhaps he is bored? Perhaps he is just trying to get attention?

What strategies did I use?

I tried to give John one of my 'looks' at carpet time. I tried reasoning with him regarding the incident with Kevin and I asked him to apologise.

What worked? What didn't work?

I just don't know what to do with John. I feel I work very hard containing him. I have tried reasoning with him, pointing out the consequences of his actions, but it does not seem to make a difference. In a sense, I feel like whatever I say is just not getting through to him. Sometimes I think I am being too soft with him.

How can I improve my practice?

Perhaps I could have done more in circle time to have prevented him from disrupting Dana. I think I should have made him apologise properly.

Secondary school

The event

Julie, who works in a secondary school, reported that she had a student who was constantly disrupting other students.

Let me tell you about a lesson with Laura in English. I was working with a group of students including Laura on looking at the character of Hamlet. The group of students were working really hard, trying to look up quotes. Then Laura's pen ran out of ink. Well, to Laura this was the end of the world. Laura screeched, 'My pen's run out of ink. Do any of you others have a pen?' At this point all the others start searching for an extra pen. I told the group to get on with the task and that I would give her a pen.

A few minutes later, Laura remarked that her old Auntie Ethel had a dog named Hamlet and didn't I think Hamlet was a strange name for a dog. Before I knew it, all the others in the group were discussing wild and wonderful names for dogs. I said that this was all very interesting but we were not doing what we were supposed to be doing. Well, no sooner had we got down to work, it must have been only minutes, when Laura's nail had broken. Actually, it wasn't broken, it was only chipped. Laura was distraught and pleaded with the other girls to find her a nail file. At this point all the other girls had tipped their bags out on their desk and were searching for a nail file. I told Laura that this wasn't the time or the place and that she could sort out her nail at break and that now she had to get on with her work.

Unfortunately, the teacher at that point asked all the students to face the front, as he wanted feedback from the class about what they had found. Our group had done very little, if any, work. I always find Laura a disrupting influence on the group. It's not that she does major things like arguing with others, or taking their pens or shoving people in line, but it is always a catalogue of little things that she does or says, or things that just seem to happen to her.

On reflection

Why do I think Laura is behaving in such a way?

Laura is just a drama queen. I don't think she means to disrupt the group. At least I don't *think* she means to, though at times I wonder.

What strategies did I use?

I constantly reminded Laura of what she should be doing and I spent a lot of time trying to refocus the group.

What worked? What didn't work?

Reminding Laura and the others only worked to a certain extent.

How can I improve my practice?

Perhaps I should be more firm with Laura? The problem is that Laura is very likeable, it is just that her head is in the clouds, so to speak. However, I don't think I am doing her any favours and I certainly don't think I am working effectively with the group.

Self-assessment questions

- What do you think are the possible explanations for Laura's and John's disruptive behaviour?
- What specific strategies do you think the teaching assistants used?
- What would you do if you were the teaching assistant?

Making sense of behaviour

Both these case studies describe students who are displaying the same inappropriate behaviour. Although we only have limited information, we can attempt to make educated guesses (based on what we have discussed about behaviour) regarding why they are doing what they are doing. Hopefully the various explanations will suggest strategies that will help to deal with this disruptive behaviour. The rest of this chapter will look in turn at the three views (behaviour determined by consequences, behaviour determined by emotions or feelings, and behaviour determined by thoughts or thinking processes) in regard to both explanations and ways forward – that is, practical everyday strategies that a teaching assistant can use.

Behaviour determined by consequences

Explanations

Here we remember that behaviour is determined by the consequences of the behaviour. One of the first suggestions from this viewpoint is to carry out a structured observation focusing on antecedents, behaviour and consequences.

Based on what we have read we could write the following analyses of John's and Laura's behaviour.

John		
Antecedent	*Behaviour*	*Consequence*
Circle time. Teacher reading story. John sitting behind Dana.	John starts to gently play with Dana's braids.	Dana turns around and tells him to 'piss off'.
	John looks all innocent.	Teacher reminds both John and Dana to listen. 'I (TA) give John one of my "looks".'
Teacher reading story.	John behaves himself for a while. John starts playing with Dana's hair again.	Dana turns around and pushes John over. Teacher asks both Dana and John to sit at the back of the class. Dana protests that John started it.
	John smirks.	
John, Kevin and Luke now engaged in group work. Kevin concentrating on writing. TA helping Luke.	John picks up his maths textbook and drops it inches away from where Kevin is working.	Kevin jumps and accidentally scribbles all over page. Kevin visibly upset. Kevin states: 'Look what you made me do'.
Others in group watching.	John replies, 'Oh does a little noise scare little Kevin?'	TA calls John over and asks him if he thought that was a nice thing to do.
Others in group watching.	He replies that it was just an accident and that he had no way of knowing that Kevin would be so scared and that he shouldn't have to say sorry as it wasn't his fault anyway. Kevin replies, 'Sorry for scaring you Kevi-poo'.	TA says that he should apologise.

The behavioural viewpoint argues that if behaviour is ongoing then there must be some sort of reward or pay-off for the student. Why is John behaving in such a way? Is John being rewarded for his behaviour?

Is John's behaviour being rewarded by attention?

John is getting attention for his behaviour, but at first glance it would seem not to be the attention a child would like to receive. John is being told off by the teacher and the teaching assistant, and his fellow pupils are angry with him. But is any attention better than none? Is being told off better than being ignored? In this short case study there is no mention of John being praised for appropriate behaviour.

Is John's behaviour a means of avoiding what he should be doing?

There is not enough information presented in the case study to answer this question. But it could be a possible explanation.

Laura		
Antecedent	Behaviour	Consequence
TA working with a group in an English lesson. Task involved finding quotes that describe the character of Hamlet. Group working quietly. Laura's pen runs out of ink.	Laura screeches, 'My pen has run out of ink. Do any of you others have a pen?'	The group stops work and begins to search for a pen. TA intervenes and tells the group to get back to work as she will give Laura a pen.
Group works quietly for a few minutes.	Laura remarks that her old Auntie Ethel had a dog named Hamlet and didn't TA think that Hamlet was a strange name for a dog.	The group discusses wild and wonderful names for dogs. TA states that this is all very interesting but that the group needs to get back to work.
Group works quietly for a few minutes. Laura chips her nail.	Laura is distraught as nail has chipped. Pleads with others to search for a nail file.	The girls tip their bags out and search for a nail file. TA reminds Laura that this isn't the time or the place and that she needs to return to work. Teacher calls the class back to discuss their group work.

Again, this viewpoint argues that if behaviour is ongoing there must be some reward for the behaviour from the student's perspective. Why is Laura acting in such a way? Does Laura really have her head in the clouds as the teaching assistant has suggested?

Is Laura's behaviour being rewarded by attention?

Laura is getting attention from both the teaching assistant and her friends. Although Laura is being told off it is in a very gentle manner.

Is Laura's behaviour being rewarded by avoiding working on the task at hand?

Although there are no comments made by the teaching assistant on Laura's interest in Hamlet, this explanation definitely seems to be a possibility. The group spent very little time on the task at hand. Despite the teaching assistant's comments that Laura has her head in the clouds, perhaps these disruptions are actually more planned than Julie imagines.

Even though both case studies describe students who disrupt other students, a careful analysis of their behaviour seems to indicate that there are differing explanations. What this shows is that writing an event in a structured format can suggest possible explanations. It is important that you discuss your observations and reflections with the teacher.

Strategies

Try to discover what is triggering the inappropriate behaviour then remove the trigger

It is possible with John that he is disruptive when he feels he is not receiving attention. One way of dealing with John's behaviour is to give him attention when he is behaving, the 'catch them while they are good' approach. As a teaching assistant this could be possible when working with a student on a one-to-one basis or within a group. Of course, it is harder to give John attention when he is sitting with a group, but it could be something as simple as a smile and a thumbs up sign when he is sitting attentively.

With Laura it is possible that her behaviour is triggered by being asked to do a task that she is unable to do or a task that she finds insufficiently challenging. Which brings us to the next point.

Play your role in making sure that tasks set are both achievable and sufficiently challenging

It is important to discuss with the teacher not only the learning objectives of the lessons but also the capabilities of the individual students whom you are supporting. Once you are aware of what a student can and cannot do, work and questions to stimulate group involvement can be considered. If Laura were asked a question on the character of Hamlet that she understood and could answer then maybe she would not need to make remarks about her Auntie Ethel's dog.

Intervene early

If the teaching assistant knows a student well, then it is possible to intervene just when you think a student is considering doing something that they shouldn't be doing . For example, after the first incident when John was pulling Dana's hair, the teaching assistant could have positioned himself closer to John. Perhaps the teaching assistant could have asked John to move? This would have prevented the later incident where both John and Dana were asked to sit at the back. The degree to which a teaching assistant can intervene needs to be negotiated with the teacher and ground rules need to be established. Should the teaching assistant have immediately involved the teacher regarding the incident with Kevin? What if the teacher was very busy with another group? Again, these issues need to be discussed with the teacher.

Likewise, with Laura, the teaching assistant could have intervened at an earlier stage. Perhaps before the students began to discuss the set task, the teaching assistant could have reminded the group that all questions and comments raised needed to concern the work that the teacher had set.

Behaviour determined by feelings or emotions

Explanations

Negative feelings, such as fear of failure are seen as threats to our self-esteem. Ways of dealing with threats to our self-esteem include becoming upset, angry or avoiding the situation.

Does this explanation fit the examples of John and Laura? Let's first look at the example of John.

On the surface John seems full of himself and he appears confident. But is he? In Chapter 2 we examined characteristics of individuals with high and low self-esteem. The characteristics of those with low self-esteem were:

- being hesitant in taking on new learning tasks, as they fear failure;
- needing reassurance – often need to be the centre of attention;
- tendency to blame other people and outside factors when things go wrong – it is never their fault;
- being uncomfortable with praise;
- being very quick to put others down as putting others down makes them feel better;
- boasting and showing off. Again, this makes them feel better.

Although the description of John's behaviour is limited, from the information available there are indicators, i.e. needing to be the centre of attention, tending to blame other people, being quick to put others down, that seem to indicate that low self-esteem could be an explanation for the disruptive behaviour.

With the limited information presented in the case study regarding Laura it is difficult to say whether self-esteem is an issue. It is possible that if her disruptive behaviour is a way of avoiding tasks that she finds difficult then there could be an underlying issue of a fear of failing.

Strategies

Teaching assistants need to be aware of all aspects of communication

They need to be aware of what they say, what they don't say and what their body language communicates. Likewise they need to be aware of what the students say, what they don't say and what their body language communicates. The way we communicate to students can be perceived as a 'put-down' or as a means of raising self-esteem.

When John states that dropping the textbook was an accident, the teaching assistant, Ryan, replies: 'I am not sure whether I believed him or not but I decided to give him the benefit of the doubt'. Although Ryan is making a real effort to believe in and work with John, is his body language communicating the same message to John? Did John feel that Ryan didn't believe him and that the teaching assistant really thought that John was a nasty piece of work?

What did Ryan really feel about John? And what if this book dropping behaviour was in fact deliberate? From what has been written it does not seem to have been an accident. Should the teaching assistant, if he thought the behaviour was deliberate, have confronted John about this? And if he had confronted John how should he have done so? Not an easy matter. Should the teaching assistant have accepted John's apology to Kevin? Should he have made John apologise again? What if Ryan still felt that John did not mean it? Should he praise John for making the effort to apologise? Such concerns are certainly issues to be discussed with the teacher.

In the case of Laura what was Julie, the teaching assistant, communicating? Julie commented that she thought that perhaps she was not being firm enough. At one point Julie states: 'I said that this was all very interesting but we were not doing what we were supposed to be doing'. Although Julie was reminding Laura about what she should be doing she was also rewarding her behaviour, boosting her self-esteem by saying that these comments were interesting. Raising self-esteem is always good, but perhaps the teaching assistant needed to focus more firmly on what Laura should be doing. Perhaps Julie could have said, 'These comments on dogs' names are very interesting but they are not helping us answer the question. In future save your comments for later and try to think of something to say about the play. I know you can make some clever suggestions if you try.'

This comment, although still boosting self-esteem, more clearly focuses on the required appropriate behaviour.

Corrective discipline should make a distinction between the behaviour and the person

This is a very hard skill to learn. In the case of John how do you tell him off, but in a way that maintains his self-esteem? Let us assume that John deliberately dropped his maths textbook to upset Kevin.

The teaching assistant could say: 'John, dropping the book deliberately and making Kevin ruin his work was wrong. I know that you can be a kind person and I expect you to try and be kind to your fellow students.'

Here the teaching assistant is giving out two clear messages: one – that the behaviour is clearly wrong, and two – that the student is really a kind person and can do better.

Teaching assistants can model emotional awareness by talking about emotions

In the case of John, the teaching assistant could try and talk about emotions. It is important to do this in private. The teaching assistant could ask John how *he* would feel if someone ruined *his* work then ask John to imagine how Kevin might feel about his work being ruined. All this requires sensitive handling which will need to be discussed with the teacher.

In the situation with Laura you could take her to one side and explain to her how her frequent disruptions make you feel.

Behaviour determined by thoughts or thinking processes

Explanations

This viewpoint states that what we do or don't do can be explained by our thinking processes. In the example of John, the teaching assistant involved, Ryan, tried to get John to think about the consequences of his actions by asking him if he thought what he had done was a nice thing to do. John didn't seem to be aware of the consequences or, if he was, he was not admitting to them. However, perhaps Ryan needed to ask John more specific questions if he wanted John to think about the consequences of his actions.

From the details in the case study it seems that Ryan had this discussion with John in front of the other students. This could have made a difference.

In the case study regarding Laura, the teaching assistant reminded both Laura and the group of what they should be doing. But could she have done more?

Strategies

Reasoning helps to develop an individual's awareness of what is right and what is wrong

Using double questions with any age group, 'What are you doing?' 'What should you be doing?', encourages students to think about their actions. Perhaps putting such questions to John and Laura would be helpful? When noticing John pulling Dana's hair the teaching assistant could have said:

Teaching assistant: John, what are you doing?
John: Who, me?
Teaching assistant: John, what should you be doing?

John:	Sitting quietly.
Teaching assistant:	Good.

When Laura is desperately searching for a nail file the teaching assistant could have said:

Teaching assistant:	Laura, what are you doing?
Laura:	Miss, my nail.
Teaching assistant:	What should you be doing?
Laura:	Looking at my book.
Teaching assistant:	When should you sort out your nail?
Laura:	At break.

Making the student aware of the impact of their behaviour on others helps them to become more aware of the reasons for rules

This strategy is more effective when conducted in private. For example, you could have the following discussion with Laura.

Teaching assistant:	Laura, how much work did we do as a group today?
Laura:	Miss.
Teaching assistant:	We didn't seem to do very much, what with looking for your pen, and nail file and talking about Auntie Ethel's dog.
Laura:	So. I can't help it if my pen runs out and my nail breaks.
Teaching assistant:	What about the others in the group? As we didn't do the work in class, you will all have to do it at home tonight. Do you think that it would be easier to do the homework if we had discussed it today in the lesson?
Laura:	Yeah.
Teaching assistant:	What can you do next time?
Laura:	Not make such a fuss.

Would this work? It is possible, but it is also possible that Laura could say that she couldn't care less if she disrupts the group and that the others couldn't care less about the homework. What then? Perhaps all you can do in such situations is what the teaching assistant did in this case study–continually try to refocus the group's attention on the task.

Self-assessment questions

- After reading the suggestions in this chapter, how would you have dealt with the disruptive behaviour?
- Think of a situation where you have had to deal with a student's disruptive behaviour. Use the techniques in this chapter to think both of explanations for the behaviour and strategies that could turn the behaviour around?

Summary

This chapter has discussed possible explanations and strategies for dealing with students who disrupt other students. In doing this we have looked specifically at two case studies. What we have discovered through this discussion is that there are a number of possible explanations as well as a number of possible strategies that can be used to deal with it. Which strategy or combination of strategies you should use in the classroom very much depends on the individual student and the particular details of the situation.

Remember

✓ Write down notes of what happened.
✓ Reflect on what has happened. Ask yourself:

- Why do I think this student is behaving in such a way?
- What strategies did I use?
- What worked? What didn't work?
- How can I improve my practice?

✓ Try to record your recollection of the events in the form of a structured observation noting antecedents, behaviour and consequences.
✓ Discuss your thoughts with others (teachers, SENCO, other teaching assistants).
✓ Look for possible explanations for behaviour. Consider the consequences, feelings and emotions, and thinking processes as being part of the explanation as well as suggesting ways forward.

Chapter 5

The student who continually talks out of turn

Students who talk out of turn pose a common problem for both teachers and teaching assistants. On some levels this is a minor behavioural problem but it can take up valuable lesson time as the next two case studies illustrate.

Primary school

The event

Nicky works in a junior school as a teaching assistant and supports a Year 5 class. Nicky describes an incident where she was working with a group of students on fractions.

> I always have difficulty with this group, or to be more specific I always have problems with Georgia. This day we were doing fractions and before we looked at the worksheet we were reviewing a few basic concepts such as numerator and denominator. I was showing the group some flashcards and asking them in turn what was the numerator and what was the denominator. The lesson went something like this:

> Nicky: (Shows the card 10/12.) Georgia, can you tell me the numerator and denominator?
> Georgia: (Takes her time, others in the group begin to shuffle their books.)
> Nicky: Georgia, I can see you are really concentrating, can you tell me the answer?
> Georgia: The numerator is 10 and the denominator is 12.
> Nicky: Well done, Georgia! (Selects another card.) Rod, can you tell me the numerator and denominator? (Shows card 21/24.)
> Georgia: The numerator is 21 and the denominator is 24.
> Nicky: Yes, Georgia, you are right, but it is Rod's turn. Remember, we are taking turns in answering the question.
> Georgia: But I was right, wasn't I, Miss? I was right!
> Nicky: Yes, Georgia, you were right, but we are taking turns. OK, Rod. What do you say for this card? Remember group, it is Rod's turn. Let's give him some time to think.
> Georgia: The numerator is 5.
> Nicky: Yes, Georgia. But, Georgia, what did I say? We take turns. The rest of the group waited quietly while you were thinking. You need to show the others the same respect that they showed you. Rod, what is the denominator?
> Rod: 10.
> Georgia: Doh, it's not 10, it's 12! This is boring!
> Nicky: Georgia!

> Anyway, at that point I decided to give up on the flashcards and move on to the worksheets.

On reflection

Why do I think Georgia is behaving in such a way?

On the one hand I know that she is just very eager to please and to show you that she knows the answer, yet she can be very cruel and insensitive to the other children. I don't know why she does it. She has taken part in social skills sessions in the past, but taking turns is still a problem. She must realise that she irritates the others?

What strategies did I use?

I praised Georgia. I tried reminding Georgia of the rules.

What worked? What didn't work?

Praise works well with Georgia. However, although I tried to remind her of the rules, I don't think I was very effective.

How can I improve my practice?

Maybe I need to be more firm.

Secondary school

The event

Amanda, who is a teaching assistant in a secondary school, was listening to what Nicky was saying and replied that she has a student who also continually talks out of turn. However, this student, Darren, was in Year 9. Amanda described a specific incident.

> Well, it was yesterday in science, we were in groups and the task was to revise for the exam. We were going over the section on plants, parts of the plant, the concept of photosynthesis. We had little cue cards and a board and dice and the students had to answer questions. In a sense it was a bit like Trivial Pursuit. The session went like this:

> Amanda: Now, you all know that the test on this section is next week. To help you revise we are going to play a game.
> Darren: Great, Miss, I like games. Can we play monopoly, cluedo and what about strip poker? What about a drinking game? (The other students laugh.)
> Amanda: No, Darren. Weren't you listening? We are going to play a game about science. Now (speaking to the group) I want to explain the rules. As soon as we go over the rules we can start. Now, this game is a bit like . . .
> Darren: Rules? Why do we have to have rules?
> Amanda: Darren! Now (speaking to the group) as I was saying, the game is a cross between Trivial Pursuit and Snakes and Ladders. When it is your turn to go you will roll the . . .
> Darren: Miss, can't we just play Snakes and Ladders and forget about this science revision. Snakes and Ladders! (All the others start joining in and chanting 'Snakes and Ladders, Snakes and Ladders'.)
> Amanda: Right, do we want to play or not? (Everyone, including Darren, is quiet.)

> Well, eventually I explained the rules and we made a start. It was Anita's turn.

Amanda: Anita, the question is: What is photosynthesis?
Darren: A new type of digital camera? (The rest of the group laugh.)
Amanda: No, Darren. Anyway can you let Anita answer?
Anita: Well, I thought it was a camera, too?
Amanda: Anita!
Anita: Sorry, Miss. Photosynthesis is a way of plants getting energy from light.

The lesson went too quickly. But things didn't improve and Darren continually talked out of turn.

On reflection

Why do I think that Darren is behaving in such a way?

Darren likes attention. I find Darren irritating, but the problem is that he can also be quite funny and if I am very honest I do like him.

What strategies did I use?

I tried reminding him. I tried refocusing the group and I eventually gave them a choice.

What worked? What didn't work?

Giving them a choice seemed effective, however the effect didn't last.

How can I improve my practice?

Maybe I need to be more firm. I don't mind a few comments, but if I am not careful these comments can take over and we just don't get things done. The others look up to Darren and admire him and they will follow along with what he does. In a sense his comments are deliberately meant to disrupt the group. I asked him one day why he was doing this and he replied that he was just mucking around and that he didn't mean any harm.

Self-assessment questions

- What do you think are the possible explanations for Georgia's and Darren's behaviour?
- What specific strategies do you think the teaching assistants used?
- What would you do if you were the teaching assistant?

Making sense of behaviour

Both these case studies describe students, though of varying ages, who continually talk out of turn. Although we only have limited information we can attempt to make educated guesses (based on what we have discussed about behaviour) regarding why they are doing what they are doing. Hopefully the various explanations will suggest strategies that will minimise their talking-out-of-turn behaviour. The rest of this chapter will look in turn at the three views (behaviour determined by consequences, behaviour determined by emotions or feelings, and behaviour determined by thoughts or thinking processes) in regard to both explanations and ways forward – that is, practical everyday strategies that a teaching assistant can use.

Behaviour determined by consequences

Explanations

Here we remember that behaviour is determined by the consequences of the behaviour. One of the first suggestions from this viewpoint is to carry out a structured observation focusing on antecedents, behaviour and consequences. From what we have read we could write the following analyses of Georgia's and Darren's behaviour.

Georgia		
Antecedent	Behaviour	Consequence
TA shows flashcard to Georgia.	Georgia looks at card.	TA states, 'I can see you are really concentrating, can you tell me the answer?'
	Georgia gives correct answer.	TA remarks, 'Well done, Georgia.'
TA shows next flashcard to Rod and asks him for answer.	Georgia answers the question.	TA remarks: 'Yes Georgia you are right, but it is Rod's turn, remember we are taking turns in answering the question.'
	Georgia remarks, 'But I was right, wasn't I, Miss? I was right!'	TA remarks, 'Yes, Georgia, you were right, but we are taking turns.'
TA continues, 'OK, Rod. What do you say for this card? Remember group, it is Rod's turn. Let's give him some time to think.'	Georgia again answers the question.	TA remarks, 'Yes, Georgia. But, Georgia, what did I say? We take turns. The rest of the group waited quietly while you were thinking. You need to show the others the same respect that they showed you.'
TA shows Rod another flashcard. Rod answers the question incorrectly.	Georgia replies, 'Doh, it's not 10, it's 12! This is boring.'	TA replies, 'Georgia!', then moves on to next activity.

This viewpoint argues that if behaviour is ongoing, as is the case of Georgia's talking-out-of-turn behaviour, then there must be some sort of reward or pay-off for the student. What then is Georgia's reward for her talking-out-of-turn behaviour? There are several possibilities.

Attention and approval from teaching assistant

The teaching assistant, on reflecting about the incident, remarked that on one level Georgia was just eager to please. Looking at the structured observation, although the teaching assistant tells Georgia off for interrupting, she usually makes a point of telling Georgia that she is right first. Perhaps all that Georgia is hearing is that she is right and the need to please or the need to be right is reinforcing her talking-out-of-turn behaviour.

Attention and approval from other students

It does not seem from what is stated that the other students give Georgia any indication that they admire her for what she is doing. In fact the teaching assistant remarks that they find Georgia irritating.

Darren		
Antecedent	*Behaviour*	*Consequence*
TA introduces the task of a revision game.	Darren remarks, 'Great, Miss, I like games. Can we play monopoly, cluedo and what about strip poker? What about a drinking game?'	Other students laugh. TA remarks, 'No, Darren. Weren't you listening? We are going to play a game about science!'
TA talking to the group states, 'Now I want to explain the rules. As soon as we go over the rules, we can start. Now this game is a bit like . . .'	Darren: 'Rules? Why do we have to have rules?'	TA remarks, 'Darren!'
TA talking to the group, 'Now, as I was saying, the game is a cross between Trivial Pursuit and Snakes and Ladders. Now, when it is your turn to go you will roll the . . .'	Darren: 'Miss, can't we just play Snakes and Ladders and forget about this science revision. Snakes and Ladders!' Everyone, including Darren, is quiet.	All the others start joining in and chanting 'Snakes and Ladders, Snakes and Ladders!' TA remarks, 'Do we want to play or not?'
(some time later) TA asks Anita, 'What is photosynthesis?'	Darren blurts out, 'A new type of digital camera?'	Other students laugh. TA, 'No, Darren. Anyway can you let Anita answer?' Anita agrees with Darren.

Again, this viewpoint argues that if behaviour is ongoing, as in the case of Darren continually talking out of turn, then there must be some sort of reward or pay-off for the student. What is Darren's reward for this behaviour?

Attention from other students

Darren is getting lots of attention from the other students. The others were laughing at his remarks. The others are following his lead, for example chanting 'Snakes and Ladders' and one other student, Anita, is agreeing, at least initially, with his definition of photosynthesis.

Attention from the teaching assistant

The teaching assistant is telling Darren off, but very gently. The question is whether Darren regards the teaching assistant's comments as a telling off or not?

Avoiding doing what he should be doing

Certainly through his distraction the group does not seem to be working very hard at the revision task. Does Darren's behaviour of continually talking out of turn mask his inability to answer the revision questions correctly?

What these explanations show is that although these two case studies detail the same inappropriate behaviour, the same behaviour could have differing explanations. All of these observations and reflections need to be discussed with the teacher.

Strategies

Try to discover what is triggering the inappropriate behaviour then remove the trigger

It could be that both Darren's and Georgia's behaviour is triggered by a great need to be the centre of attention. The teaching assistant, having realised the student's need for attention, could arrange the activity in such a manner that would guarantee that Georgia and Darren received the attention that they craved but in a manner that could be rewarded. Georgia, for instance, could be given the task of picking up the flashcards and asking the others questions. Darren could be given responsibility for ensuring that the others in the group followed the rules correctly. If Darren and Georgia carried out their respective jobs suitably they could be rewarded for their appropriate behaviour. Giving Darren and Georgia responsibility would also have the effect of boosting their self esteem.

Play your role in making sure that the tasks set are achievable and sufficiently challenging

One of the possible explanations for Darren's talking-out-of-turn behaviour was the possibility that he was avoiding a task that he could not do. As a teaching assistant it is important to get to know the students you support and to be aware of their capabilities.

Intervene early

With Georgia's group it is possible that you could arrange the activity in such a manner that the students had to write the answers to all the questions on an individual whiteboard. Then, when given the signal, the students could reveal their answers. This strategy would have several advantages. All the students would be involved in answering all the questions. This would eliminate the possibility that some students would get bored or frustrated by how long they would have to wait for their turn. This would hopefully prevent the temptation to call out the answer. However, would this prevent Georgia from talking out of turn?

Point out role models

Pointing out suitable role models is always an advantage. In the case study with Darren what has transpired is that Darren has become the role model for the others. However, his behaviour is not the sort of behaviour that you would want the others to imitate.

Behaviour determined by feelings or emotions

Explanations

Negative feelings such as fear of failure are seen as threats to our self-esteem. Ways of dealing with threats to our self-esteem include becoming upset, angry or avoiding the situation. The characteristics of those with low self-esteem include:

- being hesitant in taking on new learning tasks as they fear failure;
- needing reassurance – often need to be the centre of attention;
- tending to blame other people and outside factors when things go wrong – it is never their fault;
- being very quick to put others down – putting others down makes them feel better;
- boasting and showing off – again this makes them feel better.

Georgia's talking-out-of-turn behaviour could be explained by low self-esteem. It certainly seemed that Georgia needed to be the centre of attention, she needed constant reassurance that she was right and she was very quick to point out others' mistakes, perhaps in an attempt to make herself feel better.

In dealing with talking-out-of-turn behaviour it is important to distinguish those students who are acting in such a way because they are just eager to please from those such as Georgia who have a real need to be the centre of attention and those students who are deliberately trying to disrupt the lesson.

Can Darren's behaviour be explained in terms of feelings and emotions? Certainly we could say that Darren enjoys being the centre of attention. But is he hesitant in taking on new learning tasks, as he fears failure? The short case study does not really give us enough information. However, if you were the teaching assistant involved you would be in a position to explore possible explanations.

Strategies

Teaching assistants need to be aware of all aspects of communication

They need to be aware of what they say, what they don't say and what their body language communicates. Likewise, they need to be aware of what the students say, what they don't say and what their body language communicates. The way we communicate to the student can be perceived as a 'put-down' or as a means of raising self-esteem.

The teaching assistant in the case study involving Georgia was effective in responding to Georgia's need to be told that she was correct but at the same time reminded Georgia that her behaviour was not what it should be.

From the case study involving Darren it is not evident how successful the teaching assistant was at raising Darren's self-esteem. However, it is fairly obvious that his self-esteem is being boosted by the response he is getting from his fellow students.

Corrective discipline should make a distinction between the behaviour and the person

With Georgia, the teaching assistant tries to make a distinction between the behaviour and the person by saying at one point to Georgia, 'Yes, Georgia, you were right, but we are taking turns'. Does Darren's teaching assistant make a distinction between the behaviour and the person in telling Darren off? What Darren's teaching assistant said was:

'No, Darren, weren't you listening?'
'Darren, Now!'

'Right do we want to play or not?'
'No, Darren. Anyway can you let Anita answer?'

Could Darren's teaching assistant have corrected Darren in another manner?

Teaching assistants can model emotional awareness by talking about their own emotions and how they deal with them

This technique is often more effective on a one-to-one basis. The teaching assistant could talk about how the student's behaviour makes them feel or comment on how the student's behaviour might make other students feel. The teaching assistant could describe situations where they might have acted similarly and what emotions caused them to behave in such a manner. Let's look at some examples.

Teaching assistant: Darren, when you constantly interrupt me when I am trying to explain what we have to do, *I feel* upset.

or

Teaching assistant: I know the others laugh at your comments, but we aren't getting any work done. If we don't do the work then it will be harder for everyone to revise. How do you think *the others will feel* when it comes to revision?

or

Teaching assistant: I know that when I am in a situation that I can't handle or find difficult, I tend to ask all sorts of silly questions. I remember when I was about your age, I found maths very difficult and to get out of doing maths I would try and get the teacher talking about all sorts of other things. I would ask him how his mother was, whether he had any pets. The other students all found this very amusing but I did it just to avoid doing maths.

If we look at the example of Georgia, the teaching assistant could perhaps use the following tactics.

Teaching assistant: Georgia, how do you *feel* when you got a question right? Do you feel good?
Georgia: Yes.
Teaching assistant: Georgia, how do you *feel* when you get a question wrong? When you get a question wrong what do you want people to say to you?
Georgia: But, I don't.
Teaching assistant: If you did, what should I say? Should I be nice?
Georgia: Yes, you should be nice to me, but I am never wrong.
Teaching assistant: Do you think you were nice to Rod when he got the question wrong? How do you think Rod feels?

These examples show that it is important to try to develop an awareness of others' emotions, but that is not always easy.

Behaviour determined by thoughts or thinking processes

Explanations

This viewpoint states that what we do or don't do can be explained by our thinking processes. To what extent can thinking processes explain Georgia's and Darren's behaviour? Did Georgia think about what she was doing? Certainly the teaching assistant tried to encourage Georgia to think about her behaviour, by reminding her of the rules of taking turns and pointing out to Georgia that the group waited for her to answer and that she should show the same respect to others. However, the teaching assistant's attempts at reasoning did not seem to have any influence on Georgia's behaviour.

Likewise with Darren, the teaching assistant makes an attempt at reasoning by asking him to explain why he was behaving in such a way and by giving Darren and the group choices, i.e. 'Do we want to play or not?' The issue for both teaching assistants is whether they could have used reasoning more effectively.

Behaviour determined by thoughts or thinking processes

Strategies

Using double questions

At all ages reasoning helps to develop an individual's awareness of what is right and what is wrong, what is appropriate and what is inappropriate. Using double questions, 'What are you doing?', 'What should you be doing?', encourages the student to think about their actions.

For example, with Darren the teaching assistant could have said:

Teaching assistant:	Now this game is a bit like . . .
Darren:	Rules! Why do we have rules?
Teaching assistant:	Do we have rules about asking questions? Do we have rules about not interrupting?
Darren:	Yes.
Teaching assistant:	*What are you doing?*
Darren:	Talking out of turn again.
Teaching assistant:	*What should you be doing?*
Darren:	Listening.
Teaching assistant:	Thank you.

For example, with Georgia the teaching assistant could have said this:

Georgia:	The numerator is five. (This is the second time Georgia has talked out of turn.)
Teaching assistant:	Yes, the answer is five, but *what are you doing?*
Georgia:	Answering the question.
Teaching assistant:	But *what should you be doing?*
Georgia:	Letting Rod answer the question.
Teaching assistant:	Thank you, Georgia.

Giving the student a choice and stating the consequences

In the case study regarding Darren it is possible that Darren is deliberately trying to disrupt the lesson. If this is the case then the teaching assistant needs to be very clear about choices and consequences with Darren. Again, this type of corrective feedback is better given on a one-to-one basis as shown in the following example.

Teaching assistant: Darren, you have constantly interrupted our session. If you continue to talk out of turn I will have to report your behaviour to the teacher. Miss has already talked to you about this sort of behaviour last week and you know that the consequence for repeating this behaviour is to have a detention. The choice is yours. You either come back to the group and play the game sensibly or, if you continue to talk out of turn and disrupt the game, you will have a detention.

Summary

This chapter has discussed possible explanations and strategies for dealing with students who continually disrupt others. In doing this we have looked specifically at two case studies. What we have discovered through this discussion is that there are a number of possible explanations as well as a number of possible strategies that can be used to deal with the behaviour. Which strategy, or combination of strategies, you should use in the classroom very much depends on the individual student and the particular details of the situation.

Remember

✓   Write down notes of what happened.
✓   Reflect on what has happened. Ask yourself:

- Why do I think this student is behaving in such a way?
- What strategies did I use?
- What worked? What didn't work?
- How can I improve my practice?

✓   Try to record your recollection of the events in the form of a structured observation noting antecedents, behaviour and consequences.
✓   Discuss your thoughts with others (teachers, SENCO, other teaching assistants).
✓   Look for possible explanations for behaviour. Consider the consequences, feelings and emotions, and thinking processes as being part of the explanation as well as suggesting ways forward.

Chapter 6

The student who uses inappropriate language

Inappropriate language from students is a very common problem facing teaching assistants. Each school will have specific policies regarding what is and what is not acceptable language and teaching assistants will work within these guidelines. Two case studies that explore these issues follow.

Primary school

The event

Maya was working as a teaching assistant supporting a Year 1 class.

> Well, you know what children are like at that age. Let me tell you about yesterday. Our usual teacher was off sick and we had a supply teacher in. Well, how can I describe her? Mrs Jones, is a very well endowed woman. I was working with a group of boys, Sam, Leon, Malcolm and Ahmed. Well Sam, started it, he started whispering to the boys and they were all giggling. I asked him what it was all about and he then put two textbooks under his shirt and started wriggling them, saying : 'I'm Mrs Jones, I'm Mrs Jones'. The rest of the boys started to giggle. I put my hands on my hips and gave them a serious look. However, before I could say anything Leon remarked: 'I would like to get my hands on those'. The boys were besides themselves. I thought that was totally out of line and I reminded the boys that there was a way of behaving in class and what they had just said was inappropriate and disrespectful and that I would inform their teacher of their behaviour when she returned. Well, that certainly stopped them laughing.

On reflection

I find this a really difficult issue to deal with. It is very clear in the behaviour policy that this sort of language is not acceptable and I know that the teacher takes a firm stance on disrespectful language. I was also worried that Mrs Jones had noticed the boys' behaviour.

Why did I think the boys behaved in such a manner?

As far as Leon's comments go, well I just don't know where he heard that from. In some ways they are just at that age.

What strategies did I use?

I certainly communicated to them my disapproval by giving them a serious look and putting my hands on my hips to tell them that I was angry. I told them that their behaviour was inappropriate.

on antecedents, behaviour and consequences. From what we have read we could write the following analyses of the students' behaviour.

Sam, Leon, Malcolm and Ahmed		
Antecedent	*Behaviour*	*Consequence*
Supply teacher, the well-endowed Mrs Jones, taking the class.	Sam whispering to other boys.	Other boys giggling. TA asks them what is going on.
	Sam puts two textbooks under his shirt and starts to wriggle them, saying, 'I am Mrs Jones, I am Mrs Jones'.	The boys start to giggle. TA puts hands on hips and gives them a stern look.
	Leon remarks, 'I would really like to get my hands on those'.	The boys are beside themselves with laughter. TA tells them that their behaviour is inappropriate and disrespectful and that TA will inform the teacher when she returned.
	The boys stop laughing.	

The behavioural viewpoint argues that if behaviour is ongoing then there must be some sort of reward or pay-off for the student. The reward for the boys' behaviour is really quite obvious; their mutual enjoyment in making such comments seems to outweigh the effects of being told off. Although the boys were told off for their behaviour in the classroom this did not stop them behaving in the same way in the playground where they presumed they were out of sight of the teachers and teaching assistants.

From a social learning theory point of view there are many role models for this 'laddish' behaviour. The reality is that in today's society many such remarks about women are common. Of course, the issue for the school concerns how to deal with this behaviour within the classroom and school grounds.

Richard		
Antecedent	*Behaviour*	*Consequence*
TA sitting next to Richard and going over with him the questions the teacher had given the class to do.	Richard responds, 'I don't like f****** science and I don't want your f****** help.	TA tells Richard that his language is not appropriate and that he knows that it isn't appropriate and that TA will put him on report for his language.
Others listening.	Richard replies, 'Go on, I don't f****** care!'	TA replies, 'I never swear at you and I don't expect you to swear at me'.

continued

Others listening.	Richard replies, 'Oh yes you do, miss, you swear at me'.	The other students who are listening in to this all agree with what TA has said and tell Richard that they never hear me swear. TA then says, 'I am not saying that I don't swear, I swear as much as the next person, but I don't swear in school and I certainly never swear at the students'. TA leaves him at that point.

This viewpoint argues that if behaviour is ongoing then there must be a reward or pay-off for the student.

Is Richard swearing for attention?

Does swearing give Richard a certain 'street cred' in front of his peers? Did the teaching assistant by confronting his swearing in the presence of his classmates put Richard in a position where he felt he couldn't back down and consequently led him to swear even more? From the social learning viewpoint, such language is common within today's society, but again the issue is whether the school regards this language as appropriate behaviour. What amount or degree of swearing is acceptable in secondary school? Are there any circumstances when swearing is acceptable?

But perhaps there is another more likely explanation for Richard's swearing?

Strategies

Try to discover what is triggering the inappropriate behaviour then remove the trigger

With Richard, a clear reason for his inappropriate language could be his difficulty in doing the task at hand. This clearly relates to the next point regarding playing your role in making sure that the tasks set are achievable and sufficiently challenging. With the boys and Mrs Jones it is clear what the trigger is, but removing the trigger is not going to solve the issue of their inappropriate language.

Intervene early

If the reason behind Richard's swearing is his inability to do the task, then discussing with the teacher appropriate tasks would go some way towards eliminating his behaviour. However, in the long term Richard needs to find appropriate and constructive ways of dealing with tasks which he finds difficult.

Would it be possible to intervene early with the boys and Mrs Jones? In future, if Mrs Jones were to return to the school as a supply teacher, the teaching assistant could remind the boys that she expects appropriate language and behaviour. Of course, this would need to be expressed in a language they understand.

Tactically ignore misbehaviour

In the case study regarding Richard, could the teaching assistant have acted in any other way? Could she have ignored the swearing? Could the teaching assistant while reminding him that his language was not appropriate, i.e. 'Language, please', have given Richard time to cool down. Perhaps the teaching assistant could have said: 'If you don't want help you don't have to swear, but I will be over here if you want me'. Did the teaching assistant make the situation worse by being drawn into a discussion about whether she swears or not?

Behaviour determined by feelings or emotions

Explanations

Negative feelings such as fear of failure are seen as threats to our self-esteem. Ways of dealing with threats to our self-esteem include becoming upset, angry or avoiding the situation. This could be what Richard is doing by swearing? Perhaps Richard is swearing as he finds the work too difficult and is taking out his frustrations on the teaching assistant. Perhaps Richard is swearing because he feels embarrassed that someone has to help him with science? Is Richard the only one of his classmates that needs help? Here we are making a distinction between inappropriate language that is due to frustration and inappropriate language that is used as a form of personal abuse. Does Richard always swear? If this behaviour is unusual for him then perhaps the teaching assistant needs to ask Richard the reasons for his behaviour. With the boys, perhaps their language regarding Mrs Jones can be explained by emotions and feelings that they themselves do not understand.

Strategies

Assistance can be seen by the student as valued support or as a source of stigma or shame

This issue could certainly relate to the case study regarding Richard. If Richard does need support, maybe attention needs to be paid to the manner in which he receives support. Perhaps Richard would be better in a group situation where every member of the group received the same level of support.

Teaching assistant should try to use active listening skills

In giving corrective discipline the teaching assistant should make a distinction between the behaviour and the person. Teaching assistants can model emotional awareness by talking about their emotions and how they deal with them. To some extent the teaching assistant in the case study regarding Richard used some of these strategies, but there are a number of other ways in which she could have tackled the issue of swearing. A possible approach is detailed below.

Teaching assistant:	I take it from your colourful language about this task, that this is something you just don't want to do. (Here the teaching assistant is communicating to the student that they are listening to what the student is saying.)
Richard:	Yeah. (Looking down.)
Teaching assistant:	I know when I find something difficult, I swear like a trooper. It might make me feel better but it doesn't help me do the task. Last night I was trying to do my homework for college and I couldn't get the printer to work and my 5-year-old daughter asked if she could look at what I was doing and I just lost it and yelled at her. I know I upset her, I didn't mean to, I said sorry later, it was just that I was so frustrated that I couldn't get the printer to work. (Here the teaching assistant is trying to raise Richard's

awareness of his emotions by talking about how she deals with emotions.)

Richard, I know you try very hard in science class, and I know you don't find it easy, but saying what you did to me was not right. (Here the teaching assistant is trying to make a distinction between the behaviour and the person.)

The teaching assistant could have used the above approach with Richard. Instead, she tried to develop emotional awareness of ways of dealing with difficult tasks and the difficulty of accepting help by focusing on strengths and weaknesses, reminding Richard that everyone has things that they are good at and things that they struggle with. In this case study this approach seemed to work.

However, would this strategy work with every student? Suppose the student didn't have any area in which they naturally excelled? It would then be up to the teaching assistant to find something that the student was good at or in which they were knowledgeable. Of course, to be able to do that the teaching assistant needs to know the student well. On the other hand, is it right to boost a student's self-esteem by undermining your own – 'You can do this, but I can't'?

What could the teaching assistant have said to the boys about their language regarding Mrs Jones? The teaching assistant could have approached the situation in the following terms.

Teaching assistant:	You boys are usually very kind. What you have said are not kind words. (Here the teaching assistant is using corrective discipline and is trying to make the distinction between the behaviour and the person. She is also telling the students that the behaviour is inappropriate but in words that they can understand.)
Boys:	Miss? (Puzzled.)
Teaching assistant:	If you had said those things about me I would be very upset. (Here the teaching assistant is trying to raise awareness of others' feeling with the boys.)
Sam:	But we didn't! Mrs Jones didn't see us.
Teaching assistant:	But what if she had? Would she be upset?
Boys:	(Mumble 'Yes'.)

Say important things in private

In the case study regarding Richard, the teaching assistant had the most success when she had a heart-to-heart chat in private.

Behaviour determined by thoughts or thinking processes

Explanations

This viewpoint states that what we do or don't do can be explained by our thinking processes. Did Sam and the boys really think about the remarks that they made about Mrs Jones? Did the boys understand why they should not say those remarks? Did they understand what the teaching assistant meant by the words 'inappropriate' and 'disrespectful'?

Did Richard think about why he was swearing? Did Richard really think that the teaching assistant swore at him?

Strategies

Using double questions

At all ages reasoning helps to develop an individual's awareness of what is right and what is wrong. Using double questions, 'What are you doing?', 'What should you be doing?', encourages the student to think about their actions. Would it have helped if the teaching assistant had taken this approach when Sam was imitating Mrs Jones ?

Teaching assistant:	(Hands on hips.) *What are you doing?*
Boys:	Miss.
Teaching assistant:	*What should you be doing?*
Boys:	Work.

This strategy might get them back on task, but does it encourage them sufficiently to think about their actions? Would you need to say more and try to raise emotional awareness as in the previous section? Would this approach work with Richard?

Teaching assistant:	*Richard what are you doing?*
Richard:	Isn't it obvious?
Teaching assistant:	*What should you be doing?*

Perhaps this strategy would be useful, but perhaps it would not. What this shows is that these strategies are just guides and that any given strategy that is helpful in one situation might not be very useful in another.

Using the language of choice

This helps the student to look at the possible consequences of their actions and to think before acting. In the situation with Richard, could the teaching assistant have used the following approach?

Teaching assistant:	Richard, you know that is inappropriate language and you know that such language is not acceptable within the class. I personally find that language upsetting. If you don't stop that language I will have no other choice but to put you on report. The choice is yours. (Teaching assistant moves away to help someone else so as to give Richard time to calm down.)

In this case the teaching assistant has reminded Richard of the rules of the classroom and of the reasons for those rules. The teaching assistant has given Richard time to reflect on those rules and the consequences of breaking them. Will this work?

In the situation with the boys and Mrs Jones, the teaching assistant could have taken the following line.

Teaching assistant:	Boys, we have rules about sensible behaviour in the classroom and the kind of things we *can* say and things that we should *not* say. Talking about Mrs Jones in that way is not very nice. Mrs Jones or any woman would feel hurt if they heard what you said. I want no more silly behaviour. If you *don't* stop this, I will have to tell the teacher.

Would this work? Would you be able to give the boys such a choice, or according to the guidelines in your school's behaviour policy must *all* such incidents be reported to the teacher or a member of the senior management team?

Self-assessment questions

- After reading the suggestions in this chapter how would you have dealt with the inappropriate language?
- Think of a situation where you have had to deal with a student who used inappropriate language? Use the techniques in this chapter to think of both explanations for the behaviour and strategies that could turn the behaviour around?

Summary

This chapter has discussed possible explanations and strategies for dealing with students who use inappropriate language. In doing this we have looked specifically at two case studies. What we have discovered through this discussion is that there are a number of possible explanations as well as a number of possible strategies that can be used to cope with this behaviour. Which strategy you should use in the classroom when you encounter a student who is using inappropriate language very much depends on the school's rules regarding this behaviour, the individual student and the particular details of the situation.

Remember

✓   Write down notes of what happened.

✓   Reflect on what has happened. Ask yourself:

- Why do I think this student is behaving in such a way?
- What strategies did I use?
- What worked? What didn't work?
- How can I improve my practice?

✓   Try to record your recollection of the events in the form of a structured observation noting antecedents, behaviour and consequences.

✓   Discuss your thoughts with others (teachers, SENCO, other teaching assistants).

✓   Look for possible explanations for behaviour. Consider the consequences, feelings and emotions, and thinking processes as being part of the explanation as well as suggesting ways forward.

Chapter 7

The student who refuses to do what is asked

Most students will have days when they don't wish to cooperate. Some students will have more of these days than others. What is certain is that working with students who refuse to do what is asked is a challenge. This challenge needs to be addressed by all those involved in the school. The following two case studies will explore relevant issues.

Primary school

The event

Brenda works in a Year 3 class. She reported that she found one student particularly difficult to work with, as he never does what he is told.

> For example, yesterday we were doing a science experiment, the class divided into groups and we had to discover what various objects weighed. After we had visited all the workstations, the students had to fill in a worksheet. There was quite a bit of excitement in the class during this activity and the activity took much longer than expected. The teacher was very firm with the class in stating that all the students had to finish their worksheets before they went out to break. I sat down with Jason and said in a cheerful, no nonsense manner that we were going to get this worksheet completed. However, Jason just looked at me and said that he wasn't going to do it. I reminded Jason that the teacher had said that everyone was to fill in the worksheets. Reluctantly Jason picked up his pencil. However, at that point the bell for afternoon break went and all the other students lined up to go outside. As they handed in their worksheets to the teacher, they were allowed to go out. Unfortunately, Jason had not even started his worksheet. I got up to have a word with the teacher about Jason. That is when Jason made a mad break for it and charged out of the door into the playground. Well, the teacher, Mr Collins, quickly brought him back, sat him down and said that he must write three sentences before he went out and that as soon as he had finished I could let him go. I said 'Come on, Jason, let's do this quickly'. Well, Jason just gave me that look and said very firmly 'No'. I reminded him that he had a choice that he could do the work quickly and go out with his friends or sit in at break-time. He just looked at me and said 'No'. I then tried to encourage him and said that I would help him. I said that I would write part of the sentence and he could fill in the blanks.
>
> I know Jason has trouble with writing and I thought that this was a good compromise. Well, Jason picked up his pencil, and started to write, then all of a sudden he picked up the paper and it looked as if he was going to rip it up. Jason sometimes does this when he gets upset. I quickly grabbed the paper from him and tried to calm him down. I again compromised and said 'All right, Jason, just one word. What is the first answer? What did we first weigh?' Jason said, 'Rocks', which was the correct answer. I said, 'Well done, Jason. Now just write it down'. I gave him back the paper and he wrote the first letter, threw the paper on the ground and then he made another mad break for the door.

Well, I told the teacher what had happened and showed him what Jason had managed to do and Mr Collins just shrugged and said 'Well, at least he did something'. Jason stayed out in the playground. There was now only five minutes left and Mr Collins and I went for a cup of coffee in the staff room. Unfortunately, this was quite an average day for Jason.

On reflection

Why did I think Jason was behaving in such a way?

Jason likes to be active, he likes doing practical things, but he does not like writing.

What strategies did I use?

I tried coaxing him. I tried compromising. I tried to jolly him up. I gave him choices.

What worked? What didn't work?

Well, at least Jason did do something and I know that he does have difficulty writing. However, I sometimes feel that I spend too much time compromising with Jason and that Jason is constantly pushing boundaries to see how far he can go.

How can I improve my practice?

Perhaps I need to set more realistic targets for Jason.

Secondary school

The event

John, who works in a secondary school, told Brenda that he had a student just like Jason who constantly refused to do what she was asked. The student, Charlotte, was in the Year 7 English class that he supported.

Let me tell you about Charlotte and what happened yesterday. The class were all asked to complete some exercises from the textbook. I was circulating around the class to see if the students I was supporting knew what they were supposed to be doing. Charlotte was just sitting at her desk staring out of the window. I asked Charlotte whether she knew what she was supposed to be doing? Charlotte said 'Yes'. I asked her if she had her book. She replied, 'Yes'. I then asked her to make a start and told her that I would be back to check in a few moments.

Well, when I came back Charlotte was still staring out of the window. I got down to Charlotte's level and asked quietly if there was any problem. She replied that there wasn't. I asked Charlotte if she could please have a go at the questions and if she wanted to we could do the first question together. Charlotte replied that it wouldn't be necessary. I told Charlotte that I would be back later to check.

But again when I came back Charlotte still had not started. I asked Charlotte again if there was a problem. Charlotte said very loudly that she wasn't going to do it and that I couldn't make her. I kept calm and said that she had a choice – she either started her work now or finished it after school. Again Charlotte said, 'You can't make me do it'.

At this point I made the teacher aware of what was going on. The teacher said very calmly, 'Well, Charlotte, if you don't do the work, then you will have to stay in after school and complete it'. Again Charlotte said, 'You can't make me do it'. The teacher said to Charlotte: 'Right, I will see you later'. He then ignored Charlotte and told me to help the others.

On the way out of the classroom Charlotte turned to me and said: 'Well you got me in trouble again, didn't you!' I replied that: 'You don't need any help from me to get into trouble'. Charlotte did turn up for detention, which I suppose, is something, but she did not do her work. I just don't know how to get through to Charlotte.

On reflection

Why do I think Charlotte is behaving in such a way?

Charlotte could have been bored or she could have been avoiding the task, but sometimes I think she just can't be bothered.

What strategies did I use?

I checked to make sure that she knew what to do and that she had the right equipment. I gave her time to make a start. I asked her confidentially if there was a problem. I offered to help her. I gave her choices.

What worked? What didn't work?

I feel I gave Charlotte many opportunities to do her work. However, whatever I said, nothing was effective. I felt upset that she thought that I was just getting her into trouble. I hoped by allowing her the time to get on with the work by herself I was communicating to her that I trusted her. Obviously this strategy did not seem to work.

How can I improve my practice?

Perhaps I need to be more patient with Charlotte.

Self-assessment questions

- What do you think are the possible explanations for Jason's and Charlotte's behaviour?
- What strategies do you think the teaching assistants used?
- What would you do if you were the teaching assistant?

Making sense of behaviour

Both these case studies describe students, though of varying ages, who refuse to do what is asked. Although we only have limited information we can attempt to make some educated guesses (based on what we have discussed about behaviour) regarding why they are doing what they are doing or why they are not doing what they should be doing. Hopefully the various explanations will suggest strategies to minimise their refusal to participate and encourage cooperation. The rest of this chapter will look in turn at the three views (behaviour determined by consequences, behaviour determined by feelings or emotions, and behaviour determined by thoughts or thinking processes) in regard to both explanations and ways forward – that is, practical everyday strategies that a teaching assistant can use.

Behaviour determined by consequences

Explanations

Here we remember that behaviour is determined by the consequences of the behaviour. One of the first suggestions from this viewpoint is to carry out a structured observation focusing on antecedents, behaviour and consequences. From what we have read we could write the following analyses of Jason's and Charlotte's behaviour.

Jason

Antecedent	Behaviour	Consequence
The class is participating in a science experiment after which they have to fill in a worksheet recording their answers. It is close to afternoon break and the teacher has firmly told the class that they must finish their worksheet before they could go out. TA sits down with Jason and says that we need to complete the worksheet.	Jason says that he was not going to do it. Jason picks up his pencil.	TA reminds Jason that the teacher has said that everyone is to fill in the worksheet.
The bell for afternoon break goes. The other students line up to go outside. As they hand in their worksheets they are allowed to go out to play.	Jason (who has not started his worksheet) makes a mad break for it and charges out into the playground.	Mr Collins (class teacher) goes out after Jason, brings him back, sits him down and tells him that he must write three sentences before he goes out to play.
TA says, 'Come on, Jason, let's do this quickly'.	Jason gives TA a look and says very firmly 'No'.	TA reminds him that he has a choice that he can either do the work quickly and go out with his friends or sit in with me (the TA).
Other children outside playing.	Jason says 'No'.	TA says that she will help him. Tells Jason that she will write the three sentences and that he can fill in the blanks.
Other children outside playing.	Jason picks up his pencil and starts to write and then suddenly picks up his paper and it looks as if he is going to rip it up (as he sometimes does). Jason answers 'Rocks' correctly.	I quickly grabbed the paper off of Jason and say: 'all right Jason, just one word. What is the first answer?' TA says, 'Well done, Jason. Now just write it down.' TA gives him back the paper.

continued

Antecedent	Behaviour	Consequence
	He writes the first letter, throws the paper to the ground and makes a mad break for the door and escapes into the playground.	TA shows Mr Collins what Jason has done. Mr Collins shrugs and says, 'Well, at least he has done something'. Jason is now in the playground.

This viewpoint argues that if behaviour is ongoing, as it seems Jason's refusal to cooperate is, then there must be some sort of reward or pay-off for the student. What then is Jason's reward for his refusal to do what he is asked?

Avoidance of an undesired task and the achievement of a desired goal

From what we have read and recorded it is clear that Jason has difficulty writing and that he would much prefer to be out playing rather than writing. From this analysis it seems that every time Jason refused to do what was asked, either by making a mad break for it, refusing to write, or starting to rip up his work he was rewarded by being asked to do less and less writing. The rest of the class had to finish their worksheet before going out to play. But after trying to escape Jason was asked to write only three sentences. After several refusals and an attempt to rip up the paper (a strategy that was extremely effective), Jason only wrote one letter, before throwing the worksheet on the floor and running out to play. Jason was not brought back in and therefore from Jason's point of view this strategy of refusing to do what is asked has certainly worked.

The teaching assistant and teacher are clearly exhausted by Jason's antics. From their perspective, although Jason has only written one letter, he has certainly written something, so perhaps they think they are getting through to him. However, if Jason thinks that this strategy of refusing to cooperate will get him out of completing tasks that he doesn't like, then the likelihood is that he will continue with this strategy.

Attention and approval from others

By refusing to cooperate Jason is getting lots of attention. The teacher runs out after him and the teaching assistant sits by him, helps him with his work and tries to encourage him to work. Perhaps their attention makes Jason feel that he is important. Perhaps their attention makes him feel powerful. It is not clear from what has been written what the other students in his class make of his behaviour. It is certainly possible that if the others see that this refusal to cooperate can result in not having to do what everyone else is doing, then there may be others in the class who will start to imitate Jason's behaviour.

Charlotte		
Antecedent	*Behaviour*	*Consequence*
Class asked to complete some exercises from the textbook. TA is circulating around the room and notices that Charlotte is staring out of the window. TA asks Charlotte whether she knows what she should be doing.	Charlotte says 'Yes'.	TA asks her if she has her book.
	Charlotte says 'yes'.	TA asks her to make a start and says that she will be back in a few moments.
TA comes back to Charlotte's side of the class and notices Charlotte still staring out of the window.	Charlotte still staring out window.	TA goes down to Charlotte's level and asks her quietly if there are any problems.
	Charlotte replies 'No'.	TA asks Charlotte politely if she could please have a go at the question and offers to do the first one together.
	Charlotte replies that it won't be necessary.	TA tells Charlotte that he will be back later to check.
TA again comes back to Charlotte's side of the class.	Charlotte still hasn't started.	TA asks Charlotte again if there is a problem.
	Charlotte loudly says that she isn't going to do it and that the TA can't make her.	TA calmly tells her that she has a choice, she either starts her work or finishes after school.
Class listening.	Charlotte again says 'You can't make me do it'.	TA informs teacher of what has happened.
		Teacher tells Charlotte that if she doesn't do the work she will have to stay in after school.
Class listening.	Charlotte again says 'You can't make me do it'.	Teacher says, 'Right, I will see you later' and leaves Charlotte alone.
Students are making their way out of the classroom.	Charlotte comes up to TA and says, 'Well, you got me into trouble again, didn't you?'	TA says, 'You don't need any help from me to get into trouble'.

Again this viewpoint argues that if behaviour is ongoing, as is the case of Charlotte continually refusing to do what she is told, then there must be some reward or pay-off. What is Charlotte's reward for this behaviour?

Avoiding doing what she should be doing

This is a possibility. Although Charlotte eventually went to the detention she did not do her work. The teaching assistant did ask sensitively, at least in his opinion, if there was a problem and did she need help. Charlotte was very firm in stating that she did not have a problem and did not need help, although perhaps this was not the case. If a student is refusing to do a task because they are unable or they find it too boring, then the task can be altered. However, if the student is refusing to do the task because they just don't want to, then that is a harder issue to address.

Attention from other students

It is not clear from what is written whether Charlotte was getting approval from other students for her refusal to do what was asked. Does Charlotte feel that she has a reputation to maintain?

Attention from the teaching assistant and teacher

The teaching assistant was giving Charlotte lots of attention, again in a manner which he thought was suitable and sensitive. Did Charlotte appreciate this attention? Did Charlotte perceive the attention as suitable and sensitive?

What these observations show is that although these two case studies talk about the same inappropriate behaviour, the same behaviour could have different root causes. All of these observations and reflections need to be discussed with the teacher.

Strategies

Try to discover what is triggering the inappropriate behaviour then remove the trigger

For both Jason and Charlotte the trigger for their refusal to cooperate could be being given a task that they can't do. In the case study regarding Jason it was stated that Jason had difficulty writing. Asking Jason to quickly write the answers on his worksheet before he was allowed out to play was perhaps unrealistic. If there is writing to be done, it would perhaps be better if Jason were given as much time as possible. Perhaps he could have started to fill in the worksheet while he was doing the activity.

Play your role in making sure that tasks set are achievable and sufficiently challenging

As a teaching assistant working with a student on an ongoing basis, you are in an ideal position to comment on what you think the student can realistically achieve. It is part of your role to feed these comments back to the teacher. Students who are given tasks that are achievable and sufficiently challenging are less likely to refuse to do the task. The teaching assistant working with Jason was constantly negotiating the task. Sometimes this strategy can be effective. The teaching assistant could have acted as a scribe and written down the answers that Jason gave. Perhaps she could have written the answers very lightly in pencil and asked Jason to write over what she had written after break. Sometimes giving the student something that they find very easy to do is a good way of getting into the task. Once the student has done what you have asked, then you can praise them and ask them to do a bit more.

Behaviour determined by feelings or emotions

Explanations

Negative feelings such as fear of failure are seen as threats to our self-esteem. Ways of dealing with threats to our self-esteem include becoming upset, angry or avoiding the situation. Fear of failure could apply to the students in both of these case studies.

Perhaps for Jason the reason he has to refuse is that he can't do the task as quickly or as well as his peers. Doing nothing perhaps is better than doing something that his peers would laugh at. The teacher and teaching assistant seem to be aware of his difficulties and differentiate the task, in that he doesn't have to do as much and that he is offered support. The teaching assistant praised him when he answered the question correctly and when he made an attempt at writing. But is this praise enough to boost his self-esteem?

With Charlotte the teaching assistant was aware of the importance of being sensitive. He gets down to her level, he asks her quietly if there is a problem, he gives her time to comply with his requests. In the case study regarding Charlotte, the teaching assistant used many well-known strategies correctly. However, the strategies did not work and in fact seemed to just aggravate the situation. Here we realise it is not just what you do that is important. You need to be aware of the student's perceptions of what you do. The question is whether Charlotte sees the teaching assistant's support as a boost to her self-esteem or is his mere presence proof that she can't do the task. Unfortunately, Charlotte's view of the teaching assistant was confirmed when he said 'You don't need any help from me to get into trouble'.

Strategies

Assistance can be seen by the student as a valued support or as a source of stigma or shame

With Charlotte it certainly seems that the teaching assistant's support was not valued, even though the teaching assistant really tried to be sensitive and understanding. Possibly – and this is just a guess based on the limited information we have from the case studies – Charlotte felt that having the teaching assistant around singled her out as different, stupid or a failure. Perhaps the teaching assistant would have had more success with Charlotte if Charlotte had been working within a small group. Then, while keeping an eye on her, he could focus his attention on the others in the group and perhaps over time Charlotte would feel more comfortable with receiving support. Was this an issue for Jason? It is difficult to say from the limited information presented.

Teaching assistants need to be aware of all aspects of communication

They need to be aware of what they say, what they don't say and what their body language communicates. Likewise, they need to be aware of what the students say, what they don't say and what their body language communicates. The way we communicate to the student can be perceived as a put-down or as a means of raising self-esteem. With Charlotte, the teaching assistant was very aware of the need to be sensitive. However, Charlotte was not going to make it easy for the teaching assistant. Sometimes students have great difficulties accepting help. Sometimes when a student has very low self-esteem they can not handle praise or accept kindness from others. In such cases perhaps all that the teaching assistant can do is to be patient.

With the case study involving Jason, what is apparent is that no one asked him why he did not want to do the work or why he felt unable to do the work. Students might have a history of refusing to cooperate but it is always important to ask if there is a reason. Perhaps his grandmother had died, or his parents had had an argument before he left for school.

Corrective discipline should make a distinction between the behaviour and the person

In the case of Charlotte how do you boost her self-esteem, encourage her to take on difficult tasks but at the same time convince her that refusing to do what is asked is inappropriate? What do you, as the teaching assistant, say? How do you respond to the question, 'Well you got me into trouble again didn't you?' You could say, 'Refusing to cooperate is never helpful, I am sure if you tried you could do the work. I am here to help all students in this class.' Likewise, in the case of Jason you could say, 'Saying no, you're not going to do it, won't make the work go away. If you put your mind to it I am sure you could do it. I am here to help.'

Teaching assistants can model emotional awareness by talking about their emotions and how they deal with them

Again, this strategy often works well on a one-to-one basis. For example, if the teaching assistant working with Charlotte happened to have a quiet time together perhaps the conversation could flow as follows.

Teaching assistant:	Charlotte. I know that you were angry with me yesterday. You thought that I got you into trouble. The last thing I wanted was to get you into trouble.
Charlotte:	You said that I didn't need anyone else to get me into trouble.
Teaching assistant:	I apologise for saying what I did. I felt angry that you blamed me. I was upset as I really tried to help you.
Charlotte:	I don't need your help. I don't need anybody's help.
Teaching assistant:	We all need help sometimes. All the other students in the class need help sometimes. I need help sometimes. It is never easy asking for help. When I am driving somewhere and I can't find the place, I would rather drive for an hour looking than ask for directions. My wife just can't understand why I don't ask for help. I suppose it is pride.

Behaviour determined by thoughts or thinking processes

Explanations

This viewpoint states that what we do or don't do can be explained by our thinking processes. What was Jason thinking? Was Jason thinking, 'I know, I just have to refuse long enough and then I won't have to do this worksheet?' The teaching assistant with Jason tried to encourage thinking by using the strategy of giving choices and stating consequences. The teaching assistant said to Jason that he had a choice: he could do either the work quickly and go out with his friends or sit in at break-time. The issue is whether Jason actually completed the work as first set out by the teacher and whether he actually faced the consequences of not doing the work.

With Charlotte the teaching assistant again tried reasoning. He asked Charlotte whether she knew what she was supposed to be doing, if there was a problem and stated that she had a choice of doing her homework then or later in detention.

Strategies

Using double questions

At all ages reasoning helps develop an individual's awareness of what is right and what is wrong, what is appropriate, what is inappropriate. Using double questions, 'What are you doing?,' 'What should you be doing?', encourages the student to think about their actions.

The teaching assistant with Charlotte tried to engage in reasoning by asking Charlotte whether she knew what she should be doing. Could the teaching assistant have made greater use of this reasoning technique? He could have tried the following line of reasoning.

Teaching assistant: *Charlotte, what are you doing?*
Charlotte: *Staring out the window.*
Teaching assistant: *What should you be doing?*
Charlotte: *Working.*
Teaching assistant: *Fine.*

Perhaps the teaching assistant with Charlotte needed to give Charlotte more time to get to work. Possibly, rather than going over to her every few minutes, he could just have caught her eye and motioned for her to get to work. With Jason would this strategy, of reminding him of the task, work?

Teaching assistant: *What are you doing?*
Jason: *Nothing.*
Teaching assistant: *What should you be doing?*
Jason: *Doing the worksheet.*
Teaching assistant: *Right, well have a go.*

Sometimes reasoning with a student involves stressing the relevance and importance of the work. Sometimes it helps to point out to the student how the work they are given in school can relate to their everyday life.

Giving the student a choice and stating the consequences

In both case studies the teaching assistants used the strategy of giving a choice and stating the consequences. If this strategy is used it is important to be very clear with the student regarding what the choices are and what the consequences are. If the wrong choice is made it is important that the consequences are carried through. If the consequences are not carried through, then this strategy *will not work*.

In the case study regarding Jason, Jason was given a choice of doing his work quickly and then going out to play *or* spending all of playtime doing work. However, in this case the goal posts were constantly shifting, in that what Jason had to do in terms of work, became less and less. It is important, when you ask a student to do a task, that it is a task they *can* do. It is also important to enforce the consequences. With Jason he only managed to write one letter and then throw the worksheet on the floor before he ran out to play and the consequences, of missing a playtime because he did not do his work, were never enforced.

However, in the case study regarding Charlotte the consequence of making the wrong choice was carried through, in that Charlotte was given a detention, which she served.

Making the students aware of the impact of their behaviour on others helps them become more aware of the reasons for rules

If, after trying to reason with Jason and Charlotte, by asking them what they are doing and what they should be doing, they still refuse to cooperate, then emphasising the impact of their behaviour on others might be useful.

Teaching assistant: *Charlotte, you are saying you are not going to do your work.*
Charlotte: *I am not going to do it.*
Teaching assistant: *Do we have a rule about doing work?*
Charlotte: *Yeah.*

Teaching assistant:	The rule states that we must all try to do our work to our best ability.
Charlotte:	I am not going to do it.
Teaching assistant:	If you don't follow the rule, then should the other students follow the rule?
Charlotte:	I don't care. I am not going to do it.
Teaching assistant:	Well if no one follows the rule, then nobody would do any work. Then no one would learn. Rules are for everyone.

Would this work?

Self-assessment questions

* After reading the suggestions in this chapter how would you have dealt with Charlotte's and Jason's behaviour?
* Think of a situation where you have had to deal with a student who refused to do what they were asked. Use the techniques in this chapter to think of both explanations for the behaviour and strategies that could turn the behaviour around?

Summary

This chapter has discussed possible explanations and strategies for dealing with students who refuse to do what they are asked. In doing this we have looked specifically at two case studies. What we have discovered through this discussion is that there are a number of possible explanations as well as a number of possible strategies that can be used to cope with this behaviour. Which strategy or combination of strategies you should use in the classroom very much depends on the school's rules regarding this behaviour, the individual student and the particular details of the situation.

Remember

✓ Write down notes of what happened.
✓ Reflect or think about what happened? Ask yourself:

* Why do I think this student is behaving in such a way?
* What strategies did I use?
* What worked? What didn't work?
* How can I improve my practice?

✓ Try to record your recollection of the events in the form of a structured observation noting antecedents, behaviour and consequences.
✓ Discuss your thoughts with others (teachers, SENCO, other teaching assistants).
✓ Look for possible explanations for behaviour. Consider the consequences, feelings and emotions, and thinking processes as being part of the explanation as well as suggesting ways forward.

Chapter 8

The student who has difficulty in controlling anger

A student who has difficulty controlling their anger will be challenging to work with. Discussion and dialogue between all those involved is essential in these cases. The following two case studies will explore relevant issues.

Primary school

The event

Sophie works as a teaching assistant in a reception class. Sophie reported that she never thought that you could have serious behaviour problems in a reception class, but that was before Rebecca started.

> Well, Rebecca was a beautiful looking little girl, with wavy hair that fell to her waist. She looked like butter wouldn't have melted in her mouth, but she had a temper that was unbelievable. The last major incident started in the dressing-up corner. Well, the most popular outfit for the girls was the wedding outfit. All the girls loved dressing up in that dress. Now, that morning Amy had been first over and was wearing the dress. Rebecca marched right over to her and demanded that Amy take the dress off and give it to her as it belonged to her because she was the most beautiful girl in the class.
>
> I stepped in at that moment and told Rebecca that in class we had a rule about sharing and that right now it was Amy's turn and as for being the most beautiful girl in the class, well everyone was beautiful in their own way. Rebecca would not listen to what I had to say and started to stomp her feet. I got down to her level and said in a very calm and gentle voice that she needed to settle down. But Rebecca would have none of it. She made a grab for the dress. Amy struggled and screamed. Rebecca then pushed Amy, which made Amy scream even more and in the course of things the dress was ripped. As I was right there I spoke quite firmly to Rebecca and said that pushing and grabbing was not acceptable. Rebecca was still in a mood and turned round and called me a 'fat old cow' and kicked me in the shins. The teacher arrived by my side, grabbed Rebecca's hand and marched her to the head's office.

On reflection

Why do I think Rebecca is behaving in such a way?

My first thoughts are that she is just used to having her own way. She is definitely suffering from the 'little princess syndrome'.

What strategies did I use?

I did try to remind Rebecca of the rules.

What worked? What didn't work?

Reminding her of the rules wasn't very effective.

How can I improve my practice?

I felt I tried to deal firmly and fairly with Rebecca, but perhaps I should have taken her out of the situation earlier. But, who is to say, perhaps if I had tried that, then Rebecca might just have kicked me earlier.

Secondary school

The event

Angela works with Steve. Steve has a problem with his anger and attends the behavioural unit within the school part-time. When Steve was in mainstream classes a teaching assistant always supported him. However, as Angela noted when you were supporting Steve you always felt that you were tip-toeing on egg-shells and she imagined that was how the other students felt.

> Like last Monday in History, the class had been set some work and everyone was getting on with it. I was sitting beside Steve. Then Brad at the back yelled at Steve, 'I heard that those lads from 11b are out to smash your face in'.
>
> The teacher immediately intervened and told Brad that those remarks were not acceptable in class. There was absolute silence. But those remarks had already had their effect on Steve. I noticed his shoulders tense and his face turn very pale. I tried to keep him focused on the questions at hand and to ignore Brad's remark. I asked him questions about the task and commented on the work he had done so far. I thought that by trying to keep on the task at hand he might hopefully forget about Brad's remark. Steve answered my questions and was writing the answers that we discussed. For a while this strategy seemed to be working. Then there was a slight commotion at the back and we could hear Brad's distinctive laugh. Well that was it. Steve jumped up and in a split second was at the back of the class pinning Brad to the wall. The teacher stepped in immediately and said that he was having none of this and to put Brad down. Steve did what he was told. Then the teacher asked me to take Steve back to the unit.
>
> I said to Steve that it was time to go and he followed me, but not before he gave Brad a menacing look and kicked over a chair. Steve was quiet all the way down to the unit and once he was back in the unit I left him alone.

On reflection

Why do I think Steve was behaving in such a way?

In this incident Steve was provoked by Brad's comments. Steve was frightened.

What strategies did I use?

I was very aware of Steve's body language. I noticed how tense he was getting and I tried very hard to get him to ignore Brad and to focus on the task at hand.

What worked? What didn't work?

As Steve has a statement and is attached to the behaviour unit, there are set procedures to follow if Steve acts up. If Steve displays any aggressive behaviour in a mainstream class he is required to leave immediately and go back to the unit. In this case the procedures were followed. However, I feel that maybe I should have done more to prevent the incident.

How can I improve my practice?

Perhaps I should have intervened earlier and suggested to the teacher that I take Steve out as soon as Brad made that remark.

Self-assessment questions

- What do you think are the possible explanations for Steve's and Rebecca's behaviour?
- What strategies do you think the teaching assistants used?
- What would you do if you were the teaching assistant?

Making sense of behaviour

Both these case studies describe students of varying ages who have difficulties in controlling their anger. Although we only have limited information we can attempt to make some educated guesses regarding why they are doing what they are doing. Hopefully these various explanations will suggest strategies that will help these students in controlling their anger. The rest of this chapter will look in turn at the three views (behaviour determined by consequences, behaviour determined by feelings or emotions, and behaviour determined by thoughts or thinking processes) in regard to both explanations and ways forward – that is, practical everyday strategies that a teaching assistant can use.

Behaviour determined by consequences

Explanations

Here we remember that behaviour is determined by the consequences of the behaviour. One of the first suggestions from this viewpoint is to carry out a structured observation focusing on antecedents, behaviour and consequences. From what we have read we could write the following analyses of Rebecca's and Steve's behaviour.

Rebecca		
Antecedent	*Behaviour*	*Consequence*
Amy wearing bride's outfit.	Rebecca marches over to Amy and demands that Amy takes the dress off and gives it to her as it belongs to her because she is the most beautiful girl in the class.	TA steps in and tells Rebecca that we have a rule about sharing and that it is Amy's turn, and as for being beautiful, everyone is beautiful in their own way.
Amy still wearing bride's outfit.	Rebecca starts to stomp her feet.	TA gets down to Rebecca's level and says in a very calm and gentle voice that she needs to settle down.

continued

Antecedent	Behaviour	Consequence
Amy still wearing bride's outfit.	Rebecca makes a grab for the dress.	Amy struggles and screams.
	Rebecca pushes Amy.	Amy screams even more and the dress rips. TA speaks firmly to Rebecca saying that pushing and grabbing is not acceptable.
	Rebecca calls TA a 'fat old cow' and kicks TA in the shins.	The teacher arrives, grabs Rebecca's hand and marches her to the head's office.

This viewpoint argues that if behaviour is ongoing, as it seems to be in the case of Rebecca, then there must be some sort of reward or pay-off for the student. What then is Rebecca's reward for her outburst of anger?

Achievement of desired goal

In this example it is very clear that Rebecca has her mind set on having this dress. However, despite her outburst she does not get to wear the dress. Nevertheless, she has perhaps made her point to the others in the class, that it is her dress, that she is willing to fight for what she thinks is hers and that she does not take 'no' for an answer. Perhaps in the past Rebecca has learned that when she makes a huge fuss and gets angry she often does get her own way. Perhaps when she next demands that a fellow student give her something the student might give her what she asks for out of fear.

Attention and approval from others

Rebecca is getting lots of attention by becoming angry. Is Rebecca gaining approval from others? Is Rebecca gaining respect from others?

Steve

Antecedent	Behaviour	Consequence
Class has been set individual work.		
Brad yells at Steve, 'I heard that those lads from 11b are out to smash your face in'.	Steve's shoulders tense and his face turns very pale.	Teacher intervenes and states that those remarks are not acceptable in class.
TA asks him questions about the task and comments on the work he has done so far.	Brad answers TA's questions and is writing the answers that were discussed.	

continued

Antecedent	Behaviour	Consequence
Slight commotion at the back of the class. Brad's distinctive laugh is heard.	Steve jumps up and in a split second is at back of the class, pinning Brad to the wall. Steve does what he is told.	Teacher steps in immediately and says that he is having none of this and to put Brad down.
Teacher asks TA to take Steve back to the unit. TA says to Steve that it is time to go.	Steve gives Brad a menacing look, kicks over a chair and follows TA out of room and back to unit.	Back in unit Steve is left alone.

This viewpoint argues that if behaviour is ongoing as it seems to be in the case of Steve's difficulty in controlling his temper, then there must be come sort of reward or pay-off for the student. What then is Steve's reward for his outbursts of anger?

Avoidance of an undesired task or situation

Was leaving the classroom situation and heading back to the unit a reward? Was returning to the unit the desired goal? In other case studies we have seen that students misbehave to avoid doing a task that they find difficult. However, from what has been written it certainly seems that Steve is capable of doing the work? Perhaps in this case study it was the situation that Steve wanted to avoid. Perhaps Steve felt safer in the unit.

Attention and approval from others

Was Steve's angry outburst rewarded by the attention of others? Did Steve feel that he needed to deal firmly with Brad's comments in order to maintain a certain amount of respect or 'street cred'?

Social learning theory

Perhaps both Rebecca and Steve are imitating ways of behaving that they have seen or perhaps they have been on the receiving end of such behaviour. Perhaps they believe that this behaviour is an appropriate way of responding.

What these explanations show is that although these two case studies illustrate the same inappropriate behaviour there could be various explanations. Again, all of these observations and reflections need to be discussed with the teacher.

Strategies

Try to discover what is triggering the inappropriate behaviour then remove the trigger

It would seem that Rebecca's anger is triggered by not getting what she wants, while Steve's outbursts could be triggered by remarks or comments that he feels are not respectful. However, if these events were triggering the outbursts of anger then it would be unrealistic in these cases to try to remove the trigger. We all have to realise that we cannot have what we want all the time. We all have to deal constructively with negative comments from others.

Praising appropriate behaviour

It is very easy with students who have difficulty controlling their anger to pay them lots of attention when they are misbehaving but to ignore them when they are being good. Certainly, in the early years reward charts are used, whereby a student gains points, stars or merits for episodes when they are behaving well. When the student earns a certain number of stars or merits this then qualifies them for a special reward. As stated, this works really well in the early years, but even older students are still pleased by stickers, tokens and vouchers.

Intervene early

In both these case studies the teaching assistants felt that maybe they could have intervened earlier. If you know a student well and you know what their reactions are likely to be, then intervening before the situation gets out of hand can be a very effective strategy. With Rebecca, perhaps the teaching assistant could have intervened at the moment Rebecca was having a discussion with Amy about whose dress it was. The teaching assistant could have taken her gently by the hand and guided her over to another area. The teaching assistant could have tried to get Rebecca interested in another task. 'Come over here, I want to show you this book' or 'I have just the job for you'. With Steve's history of aggression, perhaps the teaching assistant could have taken Steve back to the unit after Brad made his initial comments about the lads from 11b.

Behaviour determined by feelings or emotions

Explanations

Negative feelings such as a fear of being beaten up, a sense that others are not being respectful, that you are not valued or not seen as beautiful, can be perceived as threats to our self-esteem. Ways of dealing with threats to our self-esteem include becoming upset, angry or avoiding the situation. Possibly, a sense that others are not being respectful could apply to both case studies.

From Rebecca's point of view she might genuinely feel that everyone should do as she says and that she should get what she wants all the time. When people don't go along with her, she sees this as a lack of respect or that they don't seem to understand just how important she is. On the other hand, although Rebecca says that she is the most beautiful girl in the class, does she really believe this?

With Steve there could be an issue of needing respect. What triggered his outburst was hearing a commotion and Brad's distinctive laugh. Brad could have been talking and laughing about him, but he had no definite way of knowing that he was.

Strategies

Teaching assistants need to be aware of all aspects of communication

They need to be aware of what they say what they don't say, and what their body language communicates. Likewise, they need to be aware of what the students say, what they don't say and what their body language communicates. The way we communicate to the student can be perceived as a put-down or as a means of raising self-esteem.

The teaching assistant working with Rebecca used specific skills in an attempt to calm Rebecca. As the teaching assistant described, 'I got down to her level and said in a very calm and gentle voice that she needed to settle down'. However, this did not seem to work with Rebecca. In reading the case study on Rebecca do you feel that the teaching assistant communicated to Rebecca that she was valued, did the teaching assistant boost her self-esteem? More importantly, did Rebecca feel that anyone was boosting her self-esteem?

The teaching assistant who worked with Steve was again very aware of body language and was certainly aware that Steve was tense. The teaching assistant cleverly tried to refocus Steve on a task that he could succeed at and praised Steve for answering the questions. Perhaps the teaching assistant also needed to praise Steve for ignoring Brad's initial comments.

Corrective discipline should make a distinction between the behaviour and the person

This carries on from the point made in the last section regarding whether it is possible to boost a student's self-esteem when they are acting inappropriately. Let's examine the following dialogue that the teaching assistant had with Rebecca.

| Rebecca: | Give me that. The dress is mine 'cause I'm the most beautiful girl in the class. |
| Teaching assistant: | Rebecca, we have a rule in this class about sharing and right now it is Amy's turn. As for being the most beautiful girl, well everyone is beautiful in their own way. |

What would Rebecca make of the teaching assistant's remarks? Would she see the remarks as a boost to her self-confidence? Let's suppose the conversation went like this:

| Rebecca: | Give me that. The dress is mine 'cause I'm the most beautiful girl in the class. |
| Teaching assistant: | Yes, you are beautiful, Rebecca, but so is everyone else in their own way. Now, as for who gets to wear the dress, we have a rule in this class about sharing and right now it is Amy's turn. |

In this example the teaching assistant is boosting Rebecca's self-esteem but is also making a distinction between the person and the behaviour. Rebecca is beautiful but she still has to share.

Teaching assistants can help students to deal constructively with their emotions

Ways of dealing effectively with emotions can be learned through social skills groups. In social skills groups, interpersonal skills such as listening, praising others, sharing and talking about how to deal with anger are discussed. Often teaching assistants are involved in running such programmes.

In dealing with Steve's difficulty in controlling his anger, one of the goals would be to teach Steve skills that enable him to deal with his anger effectively. Some programmes encourage students to recognise within themselves when they are getting angry and set up a system whereby they can tell the teacher or teaching assistant that they need time out. Some of these programmes involve the student giving the teacher or teaching assistant a red card to indicate that they need to leave the room.

Behaviour determined by thoughts or thinking processes

Explanations

This viewpoint states that what we do or don't do can be explained by our thinking processes. To what extent can the thinking processes or lack of thinking processes explain both Rebecca's and Steve's behaviour? What was Rebecca thinking of? The teaching assistant did remind Rebecca that they had a rule about sharing in the classroom. Did Rebecca understand the concept of sharing? Did Rebecca understand why following rules is important?

Likewise, did Steve understand that there were rules or codes of behaviour that needed to be followed? Did Steve think that rules were not meant for him? Was Steve thinking or was he just reacting?

Strategies

Using double questions

At all ages reasoning helps to develop an individual's awareness of what is right and what is wrong. Using double questions, 'What are you doing?', 'What should you be doing?', encourages the student to think about their actions. When dealing with students who have difficulty in controlling anger, it is probably wise to use this strategy of reasoning at the earliest indication that they are becoming tense or after they have had a chance to calm down.

Let's look at the example of Rebecca. When should the teaching assistant have tried to reason with Rebecca? Possibly when Rebecca demanded the bride's outfit from Amy. The teaching assistant could have tried the following approach.

Teaching assistant:	Rebecca, what are you doing?
Rebecca:	Amy has the dress.
Teaching assistant:	What should you be doing?
Rebecca:	Waiting my turn?

Possibly Rebecca needs reminders regarding what she should be doing. Perhaps Rebecca could wear a brightly coloured badge with 'sharing' on it. Then, when such a situation arose, the teaching assistant could perhaps point to the badge to remind Rebecca of what she should be doing.

Giving the student a choice and stating the consequences

This strategy might be successfully employed with Rebecca.

Teaching assistant:	Rebecca, we have a rule in this class about sharing and right now it is Amy's turn. As for being the most beautiful girl, well everyone is beautiful in their own way.
Rebecca:	(Stomps her feet.)
Teaching assistant:	Rebecca, you have a choice. If you stop this and wait then you can have a turn next. If you don't stop, you won't wear the dress and I will take you immediately to the teacher.

With Steve, the teaching assistant commented that when Brad made his initial remarks (regarding a group of lads who were after Steve) Steve's shoulders became tense and his face went white. At this point the teaching assistant decided to try to refocus Steve on the work at hand. But the teaching assistant could have tried a different approach. She could have given Steve choices. She could have taken him outside the classroom and tried the following line of reasoning.

Teaching assistant:	Steve, I noticed that Brad's remarks upset you and I wanted to say that you did the right thing by ignoring him.

Steve:	If he says one more thing, I will have him.
Teaching assistant:	As I said, Steve, in the lesson when he made those comments you made the right choice. If you had hit him the consequence would be that you would be the person in trouble. As it stands now Brad is the one in trouble, not you. Let's keep it that way. Remember you have a choice.

In this example the teaching assistant is making Steve aware that he has a choice about how to respond. However, the teaching assistant could give Steve a choice about whether he wants to stay in the lesson. This would give Steve a feeling of control over the situation.

Teaching assistant:	Steve, I noticed that Brad's remarks upset you and I wanted to say that you did the right thing by ignoring him. Steve, do you feel comfortable about staying in the lesson? If you don't I will ask the teacher if we can go back to the unit. You have a choice, Steve. What do you want to do?

Encourage appropriate behaviour by encouraging reasoning

Let's take the example of Steve. When Steve has calmed down the following discussion could take place.

Teaching assistant:	What was all that about with Brad?
Steve:	He was having a go at me.
Teaching assistant:	How do you know he was having a go at you?
Steve:	I just knew. I could tell by the way he was looking and the way he laughed. He was laughing at me.
Teaching assistant:	He could have been laughing about something else. (Here the teaching assistant is trying to get Steve to look at the situation from different perspectives.)
Steve:	No, miss. I know.
Teaching assistant:	How do you know? Suppose he wasn't? Even if he was, did you have to have a go at him?
Steve:	Yeah.
Teaching assistant:	Steve, what else could you have done?

A strategy involving reasoning is never easy or quick.

Self-assessment questions

- After reading the suggestions in this chapter how would you have dealt with Steve's and Rebecca's behaviour?
- Think of a situation where you have had to deal with a student who has had difficulty in controlling their anger. Use the techniques in this chapter to think of explanations for the behaviour and strategies that could turn the behaviour around.

Summary

This chapter has discussed possible explanations and strategies for dealing with students who have difficulty in controlling anger. In doing this we have looked specifically at two case studies. What we have discovered through this discussion is that there are a number of possible explanations as well as a number of possible strategies that can be used to cope with this behaviour. Which strategy or combination of strategies you should use in the classroom depends on the school's rules regarding this behaviour, the individual student and the particular details of the situation.

Remember

✓   Write down notes of what happened.
✓   Reflect on what has happened. Ask yourself:

- Why do I think this student is behaving in such a way?
- What strategies did I use?
- What worked? What didn't work?
- How can I improve my practice?

✓   Try to record your recollection of the events in the form of a structured observation noting antecedents, behaviour and consequences.
✓   Discuss your thoughts with others (teachers, SENCO, other teaching assistants).
✓   Look for possible explanations for behaviour. Consider the consequences, feelings and emotions, and thinking processes as being part of the explanation as well as suggesting ways forward.

Bibliography

Brody, G.H. and Shaffer, D.R. (1982) Contributions of parents and peers to children's moral socialisation, *Developmental Review*, 2, 31–75.

Cooley, C.H. (1902) *Human Nature and the Social Order*, New York: Scribner's.

De Bono, E. (1999) *Six Thinking Hats*, London: Penguin Books.

Department for Education and Skills (2002) Self-Study Materials for Supply Teachers: Classroom and Behaviour Management, London: DfES.

Department for Education and Skills (2003) *Behaviour management: Introductory training for school support staff*, London: DfES.

Derrington, C. and Groom, B. (2004) *A Team Approach to Behaviour Management, A training guide for SENCOs working with teaching assistants*, London: Chapman Publishing.

Eysenck, M.W. and Flanagan, C. (2001) Psychology for A2 Level, Hove: Psychology Press Ltd.

Goleman, D. (1996) *Emotional Intelligence*, London: Bloomsbury.

Gourley, P. (1999) *Teaching Self Control in the Classroom, a Cognitive Behavioural Approach*, Bristol: Lucky Duck Publishing Ltd.

Harter, S. (1982) 'The perceived competence scale for children', *Child Development*, 53, 87–97.

Hoffman, M.L. (1982) 'Development of pro-social motivation: empathy and guilt', in N. Eisenberg (ed.) *The Development of Prosocial Behaviour*, New York: Academic Press.

Hymans, M. (2003) *Think before you act*, Bristol: Lucky Duck Publishing Ltd.

Kohlberg, L. (1981) *Essays on moral development: Vol. 1, the philosophy of moral development*, San Francisco: Harper Row.

Lorenz, S. (2001) *The Support Assistant's Survival Guide*, Downright Press.

Mead, G. H. (1934) *Mind, Self and Society*, Chicago: University of Chicago Press.

Nelson-Jones, R. (1993) *Practical Counselling and Helping Skills*, 3rd edn, London: Cassell.

Piaget, J. (1970) Piaget's theory, in P.H. Mussen (ed.) *Carmichael's Manual of Child Psychology*, New York: Wiley.

Pickard, J. (1999) 'Sense and sensitivity', *People Management*, 28 October, 48–56.

Rogers, B. (2000) *Behaviour Management: A whole-school approach*, London: Paul Chapman Publishing Ltd.

West Sussex Behaviour Guidance (2000).

Zahn-Waxler, C. Radke-Yarrow, M. and King, R.A. (1979) Child rearing and children's prosocial initiations towards victims of distress, *Child Development*, 50, 319–330.

Teacher effectiveness

In June 2000 Hay McBer reported the findings of their research into teacher effectiveness to the DfEE. The report identified three main factors that affect pupil progress, and which teachers are able to do something about;

- **teaching skills**

- **professional characteristics**

- **classroom climate**

In the context of a book on classroom management, two sections are worth quoting from at length: teaching skills and classroom climate. (See DfEE: *Teacher Effectiveness. The Hay McBer Report 2000*).

Teaching skills described

In classes run by effective teachers, pupils are clear about what they are doing and why they are doing it... They feel secure in an interesting and challenging learning environment. The effective teachers whom we observed and studied were very actively involved with their pupils at all times... The environment was very purposeful and businesslike. But at the same time there was always a great deal of interaction between teacher and pupils.

High expectations

Effective teachers set high expectations for the pupils and communicate them directly to the pupils... Effective teachers are relentless in their pursuit of a standard of excellence to be achieved by all pupils, and in holding fast to this ambition.

Methods and strategies

Effective teachers employ a variety of teaching strategies and techniques to engage pupils and keep them on task ... lessons proceeded at a brisk pace... Individual work and small group activities were regularly employed as ways of reinforcing pupil learning through practice and reflection... When the effective teachers were not actively leading the instructions they were always on the move, monitoring pupils' focus and understanding of materials.

Time and resource management

Effective teachers achieve the management of the class by having a clear structure for each lesson, making full use of planned time, using a brisk pace and allocating his/her time fairly amongst pupils... Activities run smoothly, transitions are brief, and little time is lost getting organised or dealing with disruptions.

Time on task and lesson flow

> Overall, effective teachers had well over 90% of the pupils on task through the lesson, and their lessons flowed naturally to achieve a balance between:
>
> - whole class interactive
> - whole class lecture
> - individual work
> - collaborative group work
> - classroom management
> - testing or assessment

Classroom climate

The factors which pupils perceived as being key determinants of their motivation to learn were:

1 **Clarity** around the purpose of each lesson

2 **Order** within the classroom

3 A clear set of high **standards** about behaviour and achievement

4 **Fairness**

5 **Participation** in discussion, questioning, giving out materials, etc.

6 Feeling emotionally **supported** so that pupils would try new things and learn from their mistakes

7 The classroom would be emotionally and physically **safe**

8 The classroom would be exciting, full of **interest**, and stimulating

9 There is a clean, comfortable, well organised and attractive **environment**.

There can be little doubt that the Hay McBer report places a clear emphasis on classroom management. It would be no exaggeration to suggest that the teacher's role in organising the classroom is central to their effectiveness. It is no surprise, therefore, to see this appearing as a concern to be addressed at the very beginning of a teacher's career.

Induction standards

The Teaching and Higher Education Act 1998 introduced a statutory induction programme in the first year of teaching. From 1 September 1999 newly qualified teachers have to meet a set of standards for the satisfactory completion of their induction year. Of these standards, the majority relate, not surprisingly, to planning, teaching and classroom management. They include the setting of clear targets for pupil improvement, planning for effective differentiation, and securing good standards of behaviour.

Key skills

Curriculum 2000 clearly signals the importance of promoting skills across the National Curriculum. Six skill areas have been identified as key skills because of their centrality to education, work and life. These are:

- communication
- application of number
- information technology
- working with others
- improving own learning and performance
- problem solving

It is difficult at first sight to see how the development of these skills can be accommodated in an already overcrowded curriculum. This becomes even more of an issue when *Curriculum 2000* identifies five thinking skills to complement the key skills and embed in the National Curriculum:

- information-processing
- reasoning skills
- enquiry skills
- creative thinking
- evaluation skills

At Antioch New England Graduate School, New Hampshire, teachers have been addressing precisely this issue for some years. The results of their thinking are encapsulated in the **Critical Skills Programme (CSP)** currently being developed in the UK by Network Educational Press. One perspective that comes out of CSP is a recognition that critical or key skills cannot be separated from the subject curriculum. For their success it is necessary to interweave these skills with the National Curriculum subjects.

	English	Maths	Science	History	Geography	Art	Music	PE	Technology	MFL	RE
Communication											
Application of number											
Information technology											
Working with others											
Improving own learning and performance											
Problem solving											
Information processing											
Reasoning skills											
Enquiry skills											
Creative thinking											
Evaluation skills											

Much here depends on the design of curricular activities, but, equally, much depends on effective classroom management. The management of time to brief students for the challenging tasks being set for them is crucial. We know from David Kolb's work on experiential learning that having an experience is not sufficient for learning to take place. (David Kolb: *Experiential Learning: Experience as the Source of Learning and Development*. Prentice Hall, 1984). Effective learning is dependent on the learner reflecting on experience so that lessons can be learned and improvements made. The teacher's role in helping to de-brief students after they have carried out an activity again puts classroom management at a premium.

Of course, the demands that all this makes on the teacher are considerable. It requires managerial skills of a high order. The teacher's work in the classroom is extraordinarily complex. *It is very different from the layman's image of teaching.*

So the term 'classroom management' is intended to emphasise the variety and complexity of classroom life, and to focus on the wide range of managerial skills that the modern teacher needs to have. It is not a system of teaching, it is instead a systematic way of co-ordinating the variety and complexity which is inevitable in the modern classroom.

So the teacher is a manager, co-ordinating a varied and complex environment, looking constantly at the great managerial issues:

➡ setting objectives

➡ planning structures and procedures

➡ attending to communications and motivation

➡ evaluating performance

The teacher really is a manager. But lest any doubt remain, it is worth recording that the idea has actually been expressed the other way round!

Peter Drucker, the eminent management consultant and writer, was attempting to answer the question: *What does it mean to be a manager?* After considerable intellectual effort he summed it all up in this single sentence!

Being a manager, though, is more like being a parent, or a teacher.

(Peter Drucker: *The Practice of Management*, Pan, 1980)

Implementing classroom management

There are not many really new ideas in education. Most of the basic principles of effective teaching and learning have been advocated for a long time. The trouble is that a lot of the advice and exhortation stops short at the classroom door. The teacher is left with a long list of objectives and imperatives and a big task of sorting and co-ordinating.

Nevertheless, good practice is widespread. Converting teachers is not the problem. At too many educational conferences speakers are inclined to dwell on the problem of 'teacher attitudes'. While this may still be partially true, it is a smoke-screen covering the real problem.

The real problem for teachers is how to build up a wide repertoire of skills and techniques, how to organise these into useful structures and styles, and how to maximise the potential of the limited time and resources at their disposal. This is the problem of classroom management. It highlights the complexity of the teacher's work. The need for it is most apparent in the large classes of the lower school where large numbers and the immaturity of the students combine to present the biggest challenge to managerial skills.

To bring about improvements in classroom management an individual teacher can accomplish much working alone, but it is much better if a collaborative approach can be used. A team of teachers (a department or faculty, a year group) is likely to be the most effective unit, but such teams need to be supported by whole school policies and practice.

The cycle of improvement

The improvement of teaching and learning is not a one-off action. It is an on-going, cyclical activity. Within such a cycle there is a thinking and planning stage which is followed by an action stage. This is followed by another thinking and planning stage, and so on. The diagram demonstrates the components of the basic cycle.

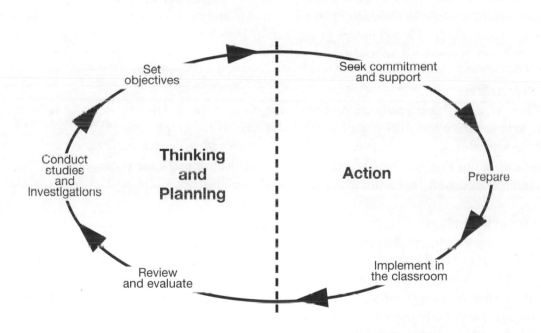

The Systematic Improvement of Classroom Management

The thinking and planning stage

Review and evaluation

This is the start of thinking and planning, and may arise out of an inspection or the school self-evaluation process. The teachers look back over the last term (or year) and ask themselves questions. What actually happened? What improvements did we succeed in making to the quality of teaching and learning? Where could we have done better? It is worth noting here that in the context of the Ofsted Framework, teaching cannot be satisfactory if any of the following is present:

- teachers' knowledge of subjects is not good enough to promote demanding work

- basic skills are not taught effectively

- a significant minority of pupils are not engaged in lessons

- lessons are poorly planned and organised and time is wasted

- there are weaknesses in controlling the class

- pupils do not know what they are doing

- pupils are not making progress

Studies and investigations

With the evaluation complete, the dissatisfactions, uncertainties, problems, and opportunities will have surfaced. Some of these may require further study and investigation. Some teachers might be asked to plan and negotiate cross-curricular work; some might study new techniques in methods or in technology. There will be visits, attendance at courses, and reading.

Objectives

The planning of next year's improvements can now go ahead. The way to use objectives is to be selective and to be practical. The question to ask is simply this: *What improvements will we see in teaching and learning between the present time and the next review?* In other words, keep it small and manageable; this is not the occasion for massive documentation or for major statements of philosophy!

The action stage

Commitment and support

The first task of the Action Stage is to get the commitment and support of people outside the team itself – students, parents, other teachers, the senior management team. By *going public* in this way the resolve of the team members becomes stronger, and much valuable advice and practical help may be obtained.

Preparation

Detailed decision-making now follows. The actual preparation may include new resources, learning activities, tests, record systems, or changes to the layout of classrooms.

The teaching

When a team of teachers has gone through this kind of collaborative preparation the teaching itself is conducted with greater resolve and mutual aid.

The benefits of the cycle

It is a disciplined way of bringing about improvements. Because it has been planned and is deliberate it serves as a constant reminder and a checklist. It focuses attention on what is important.

It is a co-operative way of working. Members of a team find it intellectually stimulating and helpful to interpersonal relations.

It introduces objectivity into classroom improvements. Teaching is such an intensely personal thing that critical analysis is a delicate and dangerous business. It is only when teachers have personally chosen objectives and gained the support of their colleagues that they will feel relaxed in the evaluation of their performance.

It is cumulative. The cycle never ends. Improvements made in one cycle become the base line for improvements in the next.

Chris Dickinson
March 2001

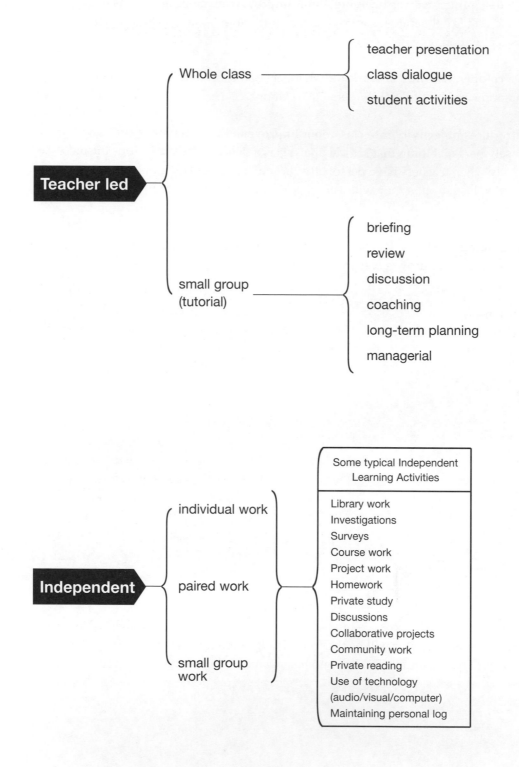

The Components of Classroom Management

A Framework for Classroom Management

> ➡ the components of classroom management
>
> ➡ the design of classroom activities

This chapter is designed to give an overview of classroom management. It provides a firm framework for the detail which will follow in later chapters.

A definition

In this chapter, and throughout the book, frequent reference is made to **'tutor'**, **'tutorial'** and **'tutoring'**. These words are intended to be understood in their original sense – referring to the support for academic learning that is given by a teacher. This is different from the use of these words in the context of personal guidance, counselling and pastoral work within the school.

The components of classroom management

One important characteristic of good teaching is its **variety**. Young people do not thrive on a monotonous diet, however well it is presented. So teachers try to vary the classroom experiences as much as possible. The range of activities is infinite, but we can put them all into two main categories:

1   teacher-led activities

2   students working independently of the teacher

The diagram opposite provides a simple classification of classroom activities. It does not claim to be exhaustive, but it will be the framework round which the following chapters in the book will be organised. The brief notes which follow are simply intended to define the various categories. Further description of techniques and styles will be given in later chapters.

Teacher-led activities

Whole class
The best known of teaching arrangements, often referred to as *traditional* teaching. When it is well done it can be very powerful and must be part of every teacher's repertoire. But that is not to say that it should be used exclusively.

> ➡ *Teacher presentation* can be very effective, provided it is used sparingly, for very short periods, and with sparkle. We must not deny our young people the

experience of being inspired and stimulated by the charisma of a really good presenter. And, happily, many teachers can provide just that.

➡ *Class dialogue*, or the so-called 'Socratic' method, is a very useful method. The teacher leads the thinking of the class by skilful questioning. It is very commonly used, and at its best it can be lively and motivating for the students. It needs careful handling, however; it can so easily lose its vitality and become somewhat mechanical and repetitive. The reader interested in developing questioning techniques is directed to Chapter 4 of *Class Talk* by Rosemary Sage (Network Educational Press, 2000).

➡ *Student activities* are important. Most teachers recognise that giving the students 'something to do' helps to bring variety into whole class teaching. The teacher remains in control of what is happening, but the students are given opportunities to be much more active. It is worthwhile making a serious study of the possibilities.

Small group work (tutorials)

It is again worth stating that the word 'tutorial' is used here to mean the academic support given to the learner by the teacher and is best understood by reference to the tutorial system of learning at Oxford and Cambridge universities.

Teacher-led tutorials with small groups are not as common as class teaching. Most teachers recognise the potential of this arrangement but are uncertain about some of the management implications with large classes and immature students. These are legitimate doubts and we shall need to examine possibilities in a careful way. But if you want to make a real difference to the quality of your students' learning, this is the way forward. So developments in this direction are worth a lot of extra effort.

➡ A **briefing tutorial** helps the students prepare for their next assignment, and gives them guidance about objectives, resources, possible problems, opportunities, and standards.

➡ A **review tutorial** looks back at work which has been completed, and provides the opportunity for reflection and assessment.

➡ A **discussion tutorial** encourages the students to talk freely about the work, exploring issues and ideas together.

➡ A **coaching tutorial** allows the teacher to work intensively to help overcome students' difficulties. With the small group it becomes possible to get to the heart of problems and to offer support which is personal and individualised.

➡ A **planning tutorial** allows students to participate in the thinking about the pace and design of the course being followed. If they share with their teacher a clear vision of what lies ahead their motivation is likely to be much stronger.

➡ A **managerial tutorial** allows students to participate in the detailed decisions about the course, decisions about resources, contacts outside the classroom, visits, special events, and so on.

Independent activities

Students will thrive if they are given a reasonable degree of independence. Indeed there is some evidence to suggest that the Key Stage 3 dip in performance is related to students losing the high degree of independence that they had in Year 6 as they move into the more controlled environment of Year 7. They need the teacher's guidance and help, of course, but they also need their own time and space, and sufficient scope for decision-making of their own. A wise teacher aims to strike a balance in order to get just the right amount of independence for each individual student.

Just as in class teaching, there is a danger of monotony. Simply getting students to work on their own is no guarantee of high levels of motivation. There is still a lot of truth in the old jibe - *Death by a thousand worksheets!*

Individual work

The opportunity to work entirely alone should be given frequently to all students. Some kinds of work lend themselves particularly well to this arrangement. Of course, good prior briefing is essential, as is the need to give additional support if it is required.

Paired work

This is very popular and needs encouragement. Friendship is normally the best basis for the pairing. It is quite easy to use the pair as the normal unit for independent work and to break for individual work occasionally, or combine with other pairs for small group work.

Small group work

At its best this is very productive. Indeed, those teachers looking to implement Key Skills in accordance with *Curriculum 2000* will be seeking to develop small group work, since **working with others** is one of the Key Skills in question. It is not easy, however. Left to their own devices many young students run into difficulties and a lot of care is needed on the part of the teacher. It is important to remember that working skilfully as a member of a small group is a fairly advanced activity – many adults can't do it! So the teacher is wise to regard the independent small group as a training ground, and to monitor progress very carefully.

Typical activities

These will not be described, since the names given on the diagram on page 18 are more or less self-explanatory. Later chapters will expand this list and discuss some of these activities in much more detail!

Design

With such a variety of activities to choose from and the desire to offer variety to the students, how are the decisions made? Is it a question of simply ringing the changes to relieve possible monotony? Or is a deliberately planned approach likely to be more effective? The latter, surely.

It is a question of deciding where each kind of activity can make the most useful contribution. Some topics and needs are best met by class teaching, others by independent work. Some are best handled by the whole class, and others by individuals or small groups. The style of the good classroom manager is that of contingency

---

management – making the methods fit the needs of the situation. The good classroom manager is not the slave of any system or method.

The diagram below suggests an outline design for the teaching of a topic.

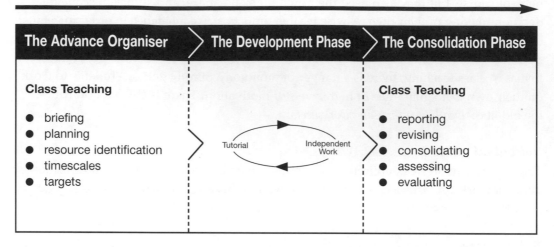

An Outline Design

The advance organiser

When a new topic is being introduced, the students need a great deal of help. Their needs are both intellectual and personal.

They need to have a vision of the new knowledge:

➡ why is it important and relevant?

➡ how does it fit in with our previous work?

➡ how will it contribute to mastery of the subject as a whole?

➡ what are the main ideas of this topic?

Remember the reference to Ofsted quoted in the Introduction; the lesson cannot be judged satisfactory if the pupils do not know what they are doing.

They also need to be inspired by the prospect of the new knowledge:

➡ to be helped to identify personally with it

➡ to have had access to clear 'images' of what the topic is about

➡ to have shared the excitement of discovering knowledge

➡ to have a sense of sharing an experience with fellow students

This is the advance organiser. It is, without doubt, the occasion for charismatic, whole class teaching. The term 'lead lesson' has often been used to describe this occasion, and in the literature of team teaching it was assumed that this would be delivered to a larger group than the conventional class and that it would be made into a very special event by the use of technology and very thorough preparation.

One such lesson, however, is not likely to be sufficient. It may be better to think of the advance organiser phase as taking up several class lessons. The first might be of the lead lesson type, but gradually the students would become much more involved as they move nearer to the next phase.

The development phase

Good class teaching needs to be followed up by well-organised independent work backed by support in small groups. A detailed discussion of the techniques and styles of this phase will be deferred until a later chapter, but some general points may be helpful now.

There will need to be a simple starter mechanism to get the two-stroke engine working. This can most easily be accomplished by gradually introducing independent work during the class teaching phase.

The students will almost certainly complete several cycles of this phase: tutorial – independent work – tutorial – independent work – and so on.

Considerable attention will have to be given to resources in preparation for this phase.

In the early stages of working this way teachers may prefer to brief the students for their independent work as a whole class. This is easier to do, and it provides a useful first step for both teacher and students. But it shouldn't prevent a march forward into the more difficult, but potentially more powerful, small group tutorial system.

The consolidation phase

After a period of time working individually, in pairs or in small groups, the students will be ready to come back together as a whole class. The style of the consolidation phase needs to be different from the advance organiser phase. Instead of relying on high quality teacher presentation, much more attention should now be paid to the contributions that the students themselves can make. It is a time for *reporting back, discussion* of issues raised, *revising and consolidating, assessing* the quality of the work done, and *evaluating* the whole topic.

So there will be heavy use of student activities organised on a class basis.

Variations in design

The outline design described above will serve well in a large number of situations. Yet there is nothing immutable about it. Two possible variations are now suggested and teachers, no doubt, will find many more.

1 Introduce the topic by getting the students to carry out a simple piece of preliminary research. Make arrangements for them to report back, and then give the class lessons of the advance organiser.

2 Divide the topic into two (or even three) parts in order to have more consolidation time. The sequence would be: advance organiser – independent work – consolidation – independent work – consolidation.

Conclusion

This chapter has served as our advance organiser for the rest of the book. It has given an outline of the possibilities. We now need to examine the detail of the various methods and techniques.

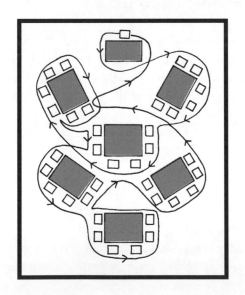

Section Two

Preparing the Classroom

➡ the organisation of space

➡ adaptations to furniture

➡ the contents of the resources areas

➡ the teacher's resources

In this chapter we consider the classroom itself. Of course it is not possible to deal with all the different situations in which teachers will be working. Many subjects require special equipment and layout, and individual rooms vary greatly in shape and size. However, it is hoped that some of the principles discussed will spark off debate as to how the work space itself can be adapted to help in the move towards better classroom management.

The organisation of space

The storage problem

We need space for two main purposes – work and storage. It is surprising how frequently the storage needs of the classroom are allowed to put pressure on the workspace needs.

Consider the traditional layout of many small classrooms. For example, in the diagram below it is clear that the amount of work space is inadequate.

working is severely restricted. No wonder that teachers working in such classrooms prefer the students to remain in their places! The trouble is that the teacher's legitimate need for storage space has been allowed to take priority over the students' need for work space.

This is a serious problem. Not only is flexible working made difficult, but the room has a disturbing influence on motivation and attitudes. There is a loss of dignity and an increase in petty irritations. What can be done? Consider the following suggestions:

Store in the classroom only those resources that are in current use

Admittedly this is a counsel of perfection. But it is an end that is worth striving for. Teachers who adopt this idea find that they prefer to store resources on trolleys so that the resources can be wheeled into the classroom when they are required and wheeled out again when they are not needed. Some organisation is needed, both in setting up the system and in operating it, but students can take on some of the responsibility.

Find space for long-term storage outside the classroom

You may be blessed with a large purpose-built storeroom or cupboard fairly near at hand. If so, consider how it may be best used. If not, you must find space. Consider the following possibilities, bearing safety regulations in mind:

➡ convert a spare cloakroom bay into additional storage space

➡ build high-level shelving above cloak racks for the storage of bulky materials not immediately needed

➡ move any slim, lockable cupboards just outside the classroom door

Find space outside the classroom to serve as additional work space

➡ if the corridor is wide enough, give it a table or bench which the students can use for noisy, dirty, or space-consuming activities

➡ convert unused cloakroom areas into extra work stations for independent work.

Alternative classroom layouts

Let us assume that we have been able to take some of the pressure off the classroom space in some of the ways described above. What alternatives are there to the traditional 'desks in rows' layout?

The 'cabaret' style

This is a splendid layout which helps the teacher to mix class teaching with student activities, either in pairs or small groups. The diagram opposite shows teams or tables of six students, but it works well with slightly larger or smaller groupings.

We shall consider the detailed operations using this layout in a later chapter.

The 'dining room' style

This focuses much more on small group activity. It can work well with students who are experienced in small group work, but it can cause problems:

➡ some students have their backs to the teacher, which is slightly awkward during longer spells of class teaching

➡ during periods of individual work students are easily distracted by students sitting opposite

The 'dining room' style is frequently found in classrooms. It is often used for small group activity, but in many situations the students sitting around the table are not required to function as a group. When this happens the arrangement is often counterproductive.

The 'workstations' style

In this arrangement the classroom is designed like a modern open plan office. Like the modern office, the classroom must provide for privacy as well as for group activity.

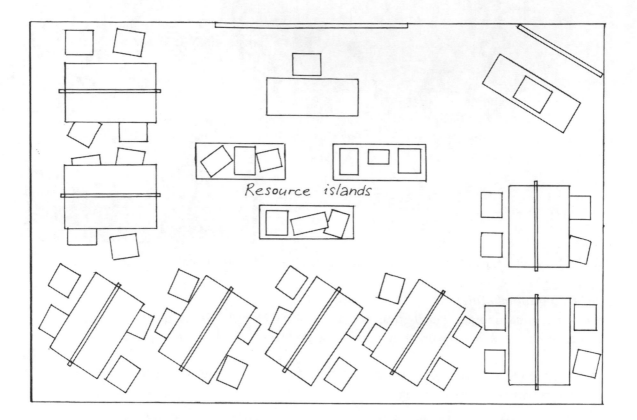

The diagram above demonstrates some of the advantages of this layout:

➡ it works quite well in class teaching; all the students can see the teacher and be seen

➡ all students can see the projection screen and blackboard

➡ because the resources are in the centre of the room, all resource-seeking expeditions are short and direct, with the minimum of disturbance for others

➡ the furniture can serve well for individual study or paired work

➡ the furniture can be quickly adapted for small group work by removing partitions

➡ the large space in the centre of the room can be easily and quickly cleared for whole-class discussions, for drama, or for any practical activities requiring space.

These are substantial advantages and it is worth a lot of effort to achieve them. Of course, much trial and error is needed to determine the best layout for any given room. Co-operation is also required among all the users of a room. The principle of students on the periphery and the resources in the centre is well worth trying.

Adaptations to furniture

In many subject areas the furniture is specialised, but where furniture is *general-purpose*, a lot can be accomplished.

The students' desks

We are assuming in our classroom that there will be a fair amount of individual or paired work. So it is worthwhile trying to improve the conditions for it. The purpose-built *carrel* or *study booth* springs to mind. This cuts out distractions and creates a private world which encourages concentration and thoughtful reflection. On the other hand it might be unwise to invest in expensive commercial products which would be heavy and inflexible in use. It is just as easy to have some simple partitions made from chipboard or lightweight fibreboard. A standard (8' x 4'/2.4m x 1.2m) sheet will make two such partitions. For safety the edges of the board should be rounded and smoothed and some simple device will be needed to make sure that the board will not fall if the tables are moved. The advantage of the simple removable board is that the arrangement can be easily switched from the ideal conditions for paired work to one large table for small group work.

The resources area

In our workstation layout this would be in the centre of the room, but is could also be conveniently sited in one corner. Ideally it would only contain resources that were in current use. If space permits it is useful to think of several small specialist areas within the one room. This has the advantage of relieving congestion at busy times. Thus there might be in a central area several resource islands, each with its own distinctive purpose.

Trolleys are valuable since the resources can be easily taken out of the room when no longer in use.

The contents of the resources area

This should contain a comprehensive collection of everything that the students are likely to need. The teacher's objective should be to have nothing to do with the organisation of the resources after the areas have been initially planned. Ambitious classrooms become very busy places with students requiring a large number of varied resources and tools. **It is fatal for classroom management when the teacher becomes addicted to helping students find what they need!** The teacher has more important things to do. So careful planning and setting up are essential.

Here is a checklist for the resource areas. Of course, each teacher must create a personal one based on subject and course needs. But this shows the level of detailed planning necessary.

Resources specific to the current unit of study

➡ printed and non-print resources organised by a simple classification for easy retrieval

➡ assignment material, carefully housed and classified

➡ test material

➡ reference material – subject reference books, dictionaries, encyclopaedias, etc.

General resources

➡ a bank of stationery – ruled paper, plain paper, graph papers, tracing paper, blotting paper, coloured paper, scrap paper.

➡ a collection of writing and drawing tools – pens, pencils, rubbers, rulers, drawing instruments, scissors, adhesive tape, coloured pencils, pencil sharpeners, masking tape.

➡ small equipment for individual or small group use – short throw slide/filmstrip projectors, slide/filmstrip viewers, audio-cassette players, personal computers. A mains cable fitted round the perimeter of the room with socket outlets just above desk-top height can be a great help.

Finally, it is worth re-emphasising the importance of good organisation. The richly resourced classroom is not necessarily the first step towards good classroom management; it can so easily become the first step towards chaos! There are a number of points to consider:

➡ Is the storage provided just the right size and so well labelled that materials can be found instantly?

➡ Can the collections of resources by checked easily and quickly when required, particularly at the end of lessons?

➡ Has a team of monitors been appointed and trained to carry out all the routine tasks that the resources system requires?

➡ Have all the students been shown the systems in operation and been given firm guidance on rules and procedures for using them?

Apply these two simple tests:

1 How many times in the course of a lesson do students put questions about the location or availability of resources to the teacher?

2 How much time during the course of the lesson does the teacher give to resources organisation?

The good classroom manager is a perfectionist in these matters and will aim to have a nil response to both questions.

The teacher's resources

It is not necessary to give detailed guidance about those resources which help the teacher to convey the message of a lesson in vivid and appealing ways. These resources are in such common use that considerable expertise is widespread. However, in the interests of giving a complete account of preparing the classroom, a few selected points are made about each of these commonly used items.

The chalkboard

It would be a pity if good chalkboard techniques were allowed to die in the face of all the new technology now available. The chalkboard is instant and in capable hands it can be very powerful. So it is worthwhile to have lots of space available, and to practise the skills:

➡ intelligent and generous use of space

➡ bold and simple graphics

➡ coloured chalks

➡ designs which allow the students to add their own contributions

The overhead projector

This is a versatile piece of equipment with some distinct advantages:

➡ With a suitably mounted screen it can provide a very large image at a great height – no problems of students not being able to see!

➡ Material (text, diagrams, maps) can be prepared in advance using computer presentation software

➡ A range of sophisticated manual techniques can be used – use of coloured pens, shading and tinting, photocopying of well-designed material, use of several layers to build up an image or to reveal parts progressively

➡ It can be used like a chalkboard to develop an explanation, but with the teacher facing the class throughout

➡ For interactive, whole-class teaching it allows students to demonstrate how they work through examples, whilst the class follows.

Television with video-recorder

The power of this combination is widely appreciated. In the hands of the best presenters it is frequently used as a serious source of raw data and stimuli rather than as a little light relief from teaching! So much use is made of the fast-forward, rewind, pause and search facilities of the recorder, as well as the on-off switch! This principle is extended in a most exciting way through interactive video.

Information Technology including Powerpoint – interactive whiteboard – National Grid for Learning

➡ Socket outlets are needed at the front of the room and at the back so that the needs of different pieces of equipment can be met.

➡ It should be possible to dim the room so that the best results can be obtained when required.

➡ Careful attention should be given to the screen – wide enough, high enough, angled against the main source of light, tilted for OHP, and with no student having to view at too acute an angle.

Audio aids

The radio and the tape recorder, used separately or in combination, add another dimension to the teacher's repertoire. Sadly they are not always fully exploited, although their value is recognised as sources of stimulating experience which will help students improve their own listening and speaking skills.

Summary

➡ The classroom must serve for teacher presentations, small group work, and for individual study. All this needs a lot of space. So it may be necessary to remove from the classroom all resources other than those in current use.

➡ Alternatives to the traditional layout of desks should be explored. The cabaret style, the dining room style and the workstation style offer good prospects.

➡ Furniture can be adapted to support the versatility demanded of the classroom. Study booths which support individual or paired work can be quickly made.

➡ The resource areas in the room should be comprehensive and thoroughly organised. The aim is to release the teacher from all resource management tasks.

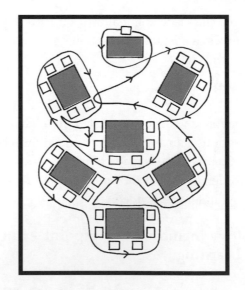

Whole Class Teaching: Exposition and Dialogue

➡ the techniques of exposition

➡ the techniques of class dialogue

We have already argued that whole class teaching plays an important part in good classroom management. Its great contribution is as an advance organiser and as a consolidator. This chapter examines what is often referred to as traditional class teaching. In this the teacher plays a leading role, relying on high quality exposition and the building up of dialogue between teacher and students.

The discussion of active learning within a class teaching mode is saved for the succeeding chapter.

Introduction

In traditional class teaching the teacher is the focus of attention, playing a number of related roles: *organiser; information giver; discussion leader.* The students are relatively passive (though not entirely so with a skilled teacher): *listening; following instructions; responding to questions; making contributions when invited to do so.*

Sadly, a lot of class teaching is dull and stifling. Critics claim that class teaching relies too much on teacher talk, that the students are not active in their own learning, that individual differences are ignored, that students are regimented in such a way as to create low motivation, poor performance, and unsatisfactory personal relationships. All this is true of class teaching at its worst, and when it is used as an exclusive method. No teacher, however dedicated, can be inspiring and stimulating for every lesson throughout a whole year.

But it is a pity when the reaction against class teaching is so strong as to imply that it has no place in the repertoire of the good teacher. In Chapter One we have described the roles that class teaching can play in a comprehensive strategy of good classroom management. *When it is not the only method in use there is less of it; and less can mean better.* Good class teaching is a vital part of the repertoire, and we must explore its potential.

The techniques of exposition

What is exposition?

Exposition is the informing, describing and explaining which is part of every teacher's stock in trade. But exposition in school is different from the set lecture which features so much in higher education. School exposition tends to be informal and spontaneous, and

---

to be very short – probably not much more than ten minutes with younger students. The exposition is invariably relieved by short bursts of other activity: a classroom dialogue, or some tasks to be done individually.

Why it is important?

Having put exposition firmly in its place as a brief and only occasional undertaking, we need now to sing its praises. It can be very attractive and very powerful. Young students still need the charisma of the good teacher. Good exposition can do all of these:

➡ motivate and inspire students

➡ stimulate their intellectual curiosity

➡ provide an advance organiser of new subject matter

➡ provide a supporting framework for a whole course of study

➡ review and consolidate

➡ make the new learning more personal through accounts which are based on first-hand knowledge

➡ give guidance to the students about the styles and techniques which are likely to be of most use in tackling new work.

When is it best used?

Exposition can take place at any time during a course of study, but it is particularly valuable at the beginning (the advance organiser), at the end (the consolidation phase), and at critical points such as topic changes or where the concepts are difficult. The 'BEM Principle' is worth recalling here: people remember more from the beginning and end of a learning experience than they do from the middle. (See Mike Hughes, *Closing the Learning Gap*, Network Educational Press, 1999.)

What should be attempted in an exposition?

If the exposition has a clear structure that the students can grasp it will stand a better chance of achieving its objectives. It helps greatly if students are invited at the very beginning to share with the teacher an understanding of the way that the exposition is going to unfold. Sometimes keeping them in the dark can be stimulating, but it can also be tiring and confusing. It is better to make the structure of the exposition explicit. The idea is similar to the advice often given to public speakers:

➡ first tell them what you are going to say

➡ then say it

➡ then tell them what you have said!

A good way of involving the students is to give them a handout which displays the structure of the forthcoming exposition and which requires some student contribution in order to complete it. A variation on this idea is to get the students to build up notes or a diagram on the chalkboard. This requires less preparation, but the students have nothing to take away from the lesson.

Examples of exposition structures

The sequential structure

In this exposition the teacher is simply explaining a sequence of events, or steps in a process, or a chain of causes and effects. The students' handout would have main headings and the teacher would pause at the end of each stage to allow a few notes or key words to be entered. Alternatively the handout could be a diagram in skeleton form which the student would be invited to complete while listening to the exposition.

The deductive structure

In this the teacher explains and justifies a set of rules or principles and then goes on to describe a number of examples or consequences derived from the principles. Again a handout would help, particularly if it allows opportunity for students to add the results of their own knowledge or thoughts.

The inductive structure

In this the teacher presents a number of examples or case studies and helps the students to arrive at generalisations or rules based on them. The exposition might have the following stages:

- briefly describe two examples or case studies
- invite students to identify similarities and differences
- briefly describe a third example
- extend the discussion about similarities and differences
- tentatively establish principles, rules, or generalisations.

Within this process there are ample opportunities for the teacher to encourage students to examine their own thought processes and the ways in which conclusions are reached. Thus the exposition makes a contribution to the students' growing intellectual maturity.

The problem-solving structure

Students like problem-solving and they will join in with enthusiasm. The exposition could go through these stages:

- state the problem as clearly as possible
- invite the students to conjecture a possible solution
- get the students to help in finding plus points and minus points for the proposed solution
- get them to make a decision. Is the proposed solution acceptable as it stands? Or does it need modifying? Or should it be rejected and a new solution sought?
- continue the process with a search for clearer definition of the problem and a number of conjectures as to the likely solution.

Problem-solving is an excellent way for the students to appreciate the provisional nature of much of our knowledge. We can only produce solutions in the light of our existing knowledge and understanding.

The compare-and-contrast structure

This is a well-tried approach in which the pupils can become engrossed in identifying similarities and differences between two sets of events, situations, or conditions. The material should be presented vividly and the use of structured notes regarded as essential.

The subject-heading structure

In the presentation of some topics students need to be given a lot of information. A clear structure with lots of headings and subheadings can be very helpful to them. There is, however, a danger of such an exposition losing its sparkle. So every effort should be made to make the ideas attractive, and to give the students something to contribute in the building up of the framework.

What are the styles and techniques of good exposition?

This is a matter of personal style and much of the technique of a good teacher is intuitive. However, techniques are worth analysing, on the understanding that the suggestions are not to be treated as rigid prescriptions for all people in all places at all times!

Get the attention of the class before you start

This can be done by a mixture of plain insistence and by giving them something to do. The latter may be little more than writing a title or an introductory statement, but it can help enormously to bring the class into the work frame of mind.

Your first sentences must be attention-holding

Appeal to their curiosity; surprise them or intrigue them; move them emotionally. Of course, it can be overdone. So sensitivity is the order of the day. But it is the mark of a skilful teacher that these attention-holding techniques can be used without alienating the students in any way. A serious and quiet sincerity can help a lot.

Keep your voice level to the minimum necessary

A low voice level creates a feeling of expectancy, gives a sense of importance to the occasion, and creates a mood of mutual confidence. It is surprising how many teachers are noisy in their classrooms. They hector their classes even when they are not quarrelling with them! A quiet teacher makes a quiet class. But even more important, a quiet teacher creates a serious and trusting atmosphere.

Vary the volume and pace to give variety

A low voice level is an excellent base on which to build some variations. To excite and stimulate the students, a different pace or a different volume is required. When students are concentrating well on the words of the teacher, a line of reasoning can be made more exciting by an increased pace of delivery; the student gets the feeling of rapid mastery of new knowledge and a sense of adventure in being able to stay with the argument.

On other occasions an appeal can be made to feelings, by a more theatrical use of language. Education is just as much about feelings as about thinking, and we should not be ashamed to express our own feelings. But these projections of the teacher's personality need to be tempered with sensitivity. Beware of over-indulgence, insincerity, and self-centred histrionics.

There is also the virtue of silence. The pregnant pause in an exposition can be effective. But sometimes silence should also be formally offered to the students so that they can reflect on weighty statements or significant problems, and consider their own responses. Throughout, the skilful teacher is able to consider the needs of the students without losing track of the development of the ideas in the exposition.

Make sure that the students never lose sight of the structure of the whole exposition.

We have already said – Tell them what you are going to say. Say it. Then tell them what you have said. It is the principle of reinforcement

It is good, too, to have frequent pauses in which a student is invited to summarise the argument so far.

Take great care in the use of language

As teachers we have to accept that in some senses our own education and training have left us with handicaps. We are subject specialists, brought up in an academic tradition, heavy users of reading and writing, and having to deal more and more with the bureaucracies of central and local government. The words we choose to use are often more suitable for academic textbooks or government reports than for speaking to a group of young people. So we need to be on our guard when talking to our students. Look our for pedantic language, avoid jargon and the language of the bureaucrat; use concrete rather than abstract words and phrases. Beware of verbosity and be alert to overworked metaphors and clichés.

Teachers need to follow three basic principles: be simple, be short, be human. In pursuit of these principles it is better to choose:

➡ the concrete noun rather than the abstract

➡ the active voice rather than the passive

➡ the short sentence rather than the long

➡ the simple sentence rather than the compound

➡ the direct statement rather than the circumlocution

➡ people as the subject wherever possible

When introducing an abstract concept it is better to start with plenty of concrete examples which are within the experience of the students. These examples provide temporary props for the new concept. Then gradually the teacher can introduce new vocabulary and more complete statements.

Remember that much communication between teacher and students is nonverbal

How you look, where and how you stand, how you move, are all observed and registered by the students. Certainly distracting habits need to be eliminated, and the confident teacher will find out from the students what these are.

But nonverbal communication is an important asset in good exposition. It can help improve the students' concentration and get more sympathetic responses. Communication by example, by signal, by gesture, should all be practised. The effective communicator can often achieve a lot without uttering a word.

The technique of class dialogue

Pure expression is not normally used for lengthy periods in the classroom for younger students. Teachers know that their span of attention has strict limits, and it is better to introduce variety with more student participation. The most common way of doing this is by setting up a class dialogue. In this the teacher leads the thinking of the class by asking questions and building on the responses received from the students. It is sometimes given the name 'Socratic questioning'. At its best it can stimulate and produce high-level thinking; at its worst it can be pedestrian and stifling. So it is worth analysing the opportunity and the possible pitfalls.

Preparation

Although class dialogue is an interactive form of learning, it does benefit from careful preparation. The teacher needs to have a mental picture of the intended build-up of knowledge and understanding. This build-up might start with familiar, concrete examples in order to establish some simple concepts. Then the question can gradually move into unfamiliar territory, towards more advanced concepts and abstract ideas. It is the lack of preparation that leads to opening questions like:

'This lesson is about the Boer War. Who can tell me what they know about the Boer War?'

The likely response is a withering silence, but even if the teacher is lucky and gets an interesting response to build on, it would have been safer to have phrased the introduction of the topic more carefully.

The planned phases of a class dialogue might look something like this.

1. Stimulus	The teacher presents a stimulus: a picture; a map, a drawing; a piece of text; a short exposition; a sound or video recording. The aim is to rouse curiosity in order to start the questioning.
2. Development	The teacher's questions help students to build upon their existing knowledge and understanding.
3. Generalisation	The teacher helps the students to recognise general statements and principles from their newfound knowledge.
4. Performance and feedback	The questions now are designed to give the students opportunities to demonstrate their understanding. They are tested on their knowledge and invited to apply it.

The questions

It is hard to prepare the exact wording of the questions in advance, and this is probably not desirable, since the questions need to be adapted to the responses being received. There are, however, a number of general questioning skills which can be cultivated.

➡ The language must be simple, clear and unambiguous.

➡ The questioning should start with an invitation to observe or identify

- The key word is what? Here are some examples…

- What are the people in this picture doing?

- What is the difference between these two shapes?

- What surprised you in this brief description?

- What is this?

➡ The questions should encourage the students to give extended answers. Consider how it might be possible to eliminate questions which can be answered simply by 'yes' or 'no', or by any single word. What? when? where? questions tend to get one-word answers. 'Do you? Don't you?' tend to get 'yes' or 'no'. Questions likely to get fuller answers often start with 'Why...?' 'How...?' or 'What would happen if...?'

➡ The questions should build up to higher levels of thinking.

The careful use of 'how?' and 'why?' and 'what would happen if?' questions can lead to students achieving these desirable goals:

➡ using evidence to come to conclusions

➡ applying rules and principles to specific instances

➡ solving problems

➡ using imagination

➡ formulating and testing hypotheses

➡ evaluation

The students' responses

Getting the best responses from the students calls for patience and skill. If we are ambitious for them we are making very big demands on ourselves. Here are some suggestions.

Be prepared to wait for an answer
If the question is greeted with initial silence there is a natural tendency to fill the gap. This soon leads to teacher domination of the proceedings and students find it comfortable to allow the teacher to provide the answers. During the silence use

opportunities for nonverbal communication. Look for the student who is on the brink of a contribution – an encouraging nod or a raised eyebrow can often tip the balance. Or try a very short prompt which will encourage the faint-hearted. Sometimes, with the right group, playing devil's advocate will relax the tension and provoke a response. But beware of saying too much! Above all it is vital to signal that you are enjoying the silence and are not in the least embarrassed, still less annoyed.

Encourage their contributions

Praise the good answers. Use the names of those who have a go. Preserve the self-esteem of those who give wrong answers by taking their answers seriously and by rewarding them with praise or a friendly gesture. Give help if it is needed during an answer. Sometimes a single-word prompt or a helpful rephrasing, even just a nod, will encourage a student to press on. The skill is to know when to withdraw.

Try to get contributions from as many students as possible

Responding only to the raised hands of the bright and eager tends to focus attention on them at the expense of all the others. So while they must be allowed their fair share, opportunity must be found to get some of the others active. A particularly reluctant student can be helped by being nominated to answer an easy question before the question is asked.

Encourage a response which expresses the personal thoughts or feelings of the student

The classroom is a very public place where thoughtfulness and sensitivity often get a poor deal. This is a pity, knowing what we now know about the place of emotional intelligence in effective learning. A quiet and serious style helps the teacher overcome this, particularly if the teacher also has the confidence to demonstrate personally the thoughtful reflection and sensitive response as an example for the students.

Encourage the response which is bold and imaginative

Even if it is incorrect, such a response must be given praise. Intellectual boldness and imagination should be given status in the classroom, and it is worth devoting time to encouraging it.

Encourage respect for the contribution of others

Set a good example of courtesy, respect and constructiveness. Then expect it of the students. Do not tolerate sarcasm, mockery, aggression or destructive criticism.

Discussion techniques

Effective questioning naturally leads into class discussion. There is no clear boundary between the two. However, it has to be conceded that the average class is far too big to operate successfully as a discussion group. So class discussion is best thought of as a variant of teacher questioning.

So the teacher should expect to be in firm control. The rules for the discussion should be clearly established and the rules of procedure laid down. In line with classroom management tools developed as part of the Critical Skills Programme, students are asked to identify their quality standards for group discussion. This can take the form of the teacher asking the question, 'What does a high quality discussion look like and sound like?' Answers can be recorded on a flipchart and kept for reference in future class discussions.

Once the housekeeping has been properly arranged, the teacher, in the role of discussion leader, needs to exercise a *democratic* rather than an *authoritarian* style. All the techniques of skilful questioning need to be used with the additional style of withdrawal into neutrality. Student contributions must be encouraged with reinforcement, prompting, and occasional summaries as to where the discussion has reached.

It is wise to set a strict time limit to a discussion and to bring it to a satisfactory close by summarising the main points made and conclusions reached. Discussion techniques are particularly useful for objectives concerned with personal attitudes, and for those concerned with problem-solving.

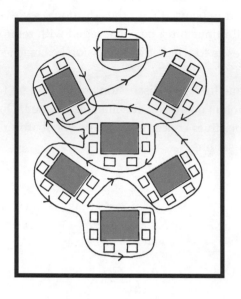

Whole Class Teaching: Active Learning

> ➡ setting the scene for active learning
>
> ➡ the techniques of active learning

There is no reason why whole class teaching should be regarded as exclusively didactic. Students can learn in active ways when they are working as a whole class.

We need active learning within whole class teaching, not only for the variety it brings. Active learning gives young students a valuable training: they are learning to make the decisions of the responsible learner, but always under the supervision and guidance of the teacher.

Active learning offers the best way of moving a programme of work from the didactic towards the more independent styles. It is a perfect tool for making what could be a difficult transition. Most teachers make considerable use of active methods during whole class teaching. Their interest in active methods is more likely to be concerned with improvement rather than with an entirely new set of techniques.

Setting the scene for active learning

Active learning techniques can be easily introduced without any special preparations, but there are some distinct advantages in thinking ahead about things like classroom layout and group dynamics.

Classroom layout

We have already argued the weaknesses of the traditional desks-in rows arrangement of furniture. These become even more apparent when active learning techniques are being tried. Active learning thrives best with:

➡ plenty of space so that activities other than reading, writing and listening can be considered

➡ a flexible layout so that the students can, when required, collaborate with each other, either as members of a small group or simply in pairs

➡ a layout which also allows the teacher to direct the activities of the whole class and, when necessary, revert to short sessions of exposition or class dialogue

These conditions are not met where the traditional layout is used. In order to illustrate the possibilities for active learning with the whole class we shall use the cabaret style of layout described in Chapter 2. This does a much better job than desks in rows. In the 'cabaret' the students all face the teacher, and exposition and class dialogue can be easily done. The grouping of the students means that the whole class can switch instantly into the very short sessions of group collaboration that this method requires. But the real benefit of a cabaret layout is that the teacher can switch quickly from one mode to another.

The role of the team in active learning

In the cabaret layout the class is organised into teams. The members of each team share a table, but sit only on three sides of it, so that they can easily attend to the teacher at the front of the class.

The size of the team

What is the optimum size of a team? As the table shows, we are trying to strike a balance. The best balance is probably achieved with teams in the range four to eight students. The team is large enough to produce a variety of opinions and responses, and yet small enough to give each student a sense of belonging.

	Large Team	Small Team
Level of student participation	Each student only gets a small share of the action	Each student gets a bigger share of the action
Range of opinions and responses brought to the discussions	Varied and therefore stimulating	Probably inadequate

It is an advantage if each team consists of an even number of students (four or six are most likely, but eight is possible). This allows the teacher the option of setting activities for pairs or for the whole team. In fact, a common approach will be to start an activity with paired work and then take the results or conclusions to the whole group.

Generally speaking it is a good principle to keep the number of teams down to the minimum possible. For example, a class of 30 students would only require five teams if the team size was six

The composition of the team

It is difficult to establish general rules. Much depends on the age and experience of the students, the spread of subject ability within the class, and the subject matter being taught. However, a few general points can be made.

➡ Attempts at rigid streaming will have a particularly adverse effect on the least able team; it will present the teacher with an uphill struggle. Overlapping should work better.

➡ There is a lot to be said for letting friendship play at least some part in the formation of the team. A good way is to start by inviting the students to choose partners for paired work, and then to form the teams from the pairs.

➡ The team can be of mixed gender. An increasing number of schools are using this strategy as part of their approach to raising boys' achievement. But there are undoubtedly some circumstances when single sex teams may be more helpful. It can be in the interest of girls to have single sex groups for practical activities.

➡ Sometimes it is wise to allow the shy and retiring students to form a team of their own. They will not be submerged, but encouraged to assume responsibility within the team.

But, it is worth repeating, there are no universal rules and teachers should make their own decisions according to the logic of their own situations.

The functions of the team

As the teams operate, the teacher can switch easily between exposition, questions, dialogue, paired work and small group work. Team activity can become an important feature of classroom work. No longer does the teacher have to keep the attention of all the students all the time. Teacher input can be sensibly punctuated by requests to teams to consider their response to questions. This is much easier than the traditional form of class dialogue, and it also has the virtue of giving every student the opportunity to participate, but without having to go public every time a contribution is made.

Teams will be effective only if some ground work has been done. The identity and importance of each team must be firmly established. We are talking about pride, loyalty, mutual support, determination to succeed. So there is a need for team building. Within the Critical Skills Programme referred to in the Introduction, students are taken through an exercise to identify quality criteria for small group work prior to engaging in it. This might simply take the form of asking them to list what a high quality team 'looks and sounds like'.

Do not regard team building as a one-off exercise, to be attended to before the serious work starts. Developing these interpersonal skills requires persistence and a certain amount of opportunism. Some things, obviously, need to be attended to at the outset, but thereafter the training will be ad hoc, learning on the job. Consider these ideas for team building:

➡ **Give the team a short lifespan**. Give careful thought to the life-span of the team. It is obviously not wise to keep chopping and changing, but permanent teams may not be the best solution. It is worth trying a short lifespan just to serve a specific part of a programme of study. If the team starts with a clearly defined task to be tackled within a definite time, this helps build the sense of team identity and removes the feeling of being locked indefinitely into a grouping which an individual may, for some reason, find uncomfortable.

➡ **Give every team member a job**. Every member should have a job and be answerable to the team. There might be a chairperson (decides agenda and keeps order during discussion), a secretary (writes down decisions or information), a spokesperson (speaks on behalf of the team), a resources officer (makes sure that team members have the resources they need), a record keeper (keeps records of achievements – both for individuals and for the whole team). Of course, different subjects may need different jobs; the examples given are simply for illustration. The jobs should be rotated fairly frequently.

➡ **Emphasise that they are there to help each other**. All team members should know that help for other members is not only allowed, but actively encouraged. That is what teams are for.

➡ **Recognise the teams' successes**. With the previous principle in mind, publicise and record team members' achievements, not individually, but as sum totals for the team (like the old systems of house points!), perhaps not all the time, but whenever possible.

➡ **Reward them as a team**. Rewards, perks, and light relief should be given on a team basis; likewise any minor sanctions!

➡ **Train them as a team**. Take every opportunity to train them in their roles and responsibilities as team members. It will yield dividends.

➡ **Lead them towards self-management**. With a sensible eye on what can reasonably be expected of the team in terms of their age and experience, encourage them to take responsibility for their own team building.

Finding a place for active learning

There are many ways in which active learning can be absorbed into a programme of work. A most common sequence is shown below. Opportunities during class lessons are so varied that it would be wrong to imply that any one sequence is better than another. On one day a class may be happy with a more extended exposition and a small amount of class dialogue. On another day, or with another topic, it might pay to get them quickly into team activity in order to keep them alert and involved. The skilful teacher uses flair, not a set of mechanical prescriptions.

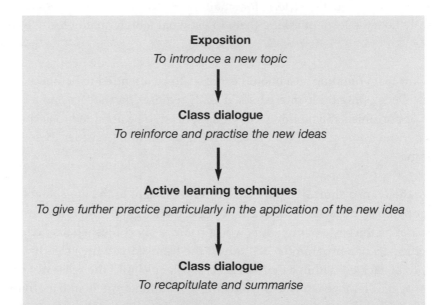

Exposition
To introduce a new topic

↓

Class dialogue
To reinforce and practise the new ideas

↓

Active learning techniques
To give further practice particularly in the application of the new idea

↓

Class dialogue
To recapitulate and summarise

The benefits of the team approach soon become apparent. Questions directed at pairs or at teams can anticipate longer, more thoughtful answers, the result of deliberation. This overcomes the main weakness of the class dialogue, which can so easily degenerate into a kind of rapid fire – a succession of short questions, with one-word answers supplied by the bright and eager, and the teacher jumping from one student to another in search of the right answer. In the team approach everyone can take part, different solutions can be explored and students learn to justify their arguments to their fellow team members.

The techniques of active learning

There is no set sequence for the techniques of active learning. Use them according to your judgement about how the lesson is progressing. Most of the techniques described in what follows are small-scale, and many are well-known. However, it is useful to build up a repertoire as a checklist so that a wide range can be used. Use the list of suggestions given here as a basis for a larger, more personal checklist. Of course, you will use more than one technique at a time. Many of them complement each other.

Snowball	Let the first thinking about an issue or problem be done by individuals (perhaps resulting in a few rough notes). Then each student shares this with a partner. Finally each pair reports to the team in order to arrive (if possible) at a team decision.
Flip chart	Whenever teams are asked to consider a problem or issue, invite them each to enter on the flip chart (or chalkboard) a single word which neatly summarises their proposed solution. When all teams have entered their word, each team is invited to explain what its chosen word is intended to convey. An alternative is to let the teams contribute to the building up of a mindmap on the flip chart.
Handouts	Handouts always useful. But they mustn't do all the work – leave something for the students to do: notes, labels, completion. Often simply providing headings and spaces in which to write or draw is all that is needed. Give them time to do their bit. Encourage them to discuss what they are doing with each other.
Library copies	Make sure that the library has a copy of anything that you consider is important in the programme of study. For example, your important introduction to a topic could have been taped and a copy placed in the library, together with any illustrations which may have been used. Encourage the students to use this facility. (*Note*: simply tape your exposition as it occurs; they will accept it as such without elaborate editing.)
Review	It is often helpful to start a lesson with a quick review of what happened in the last lesson – but make this the first job, on arrival, of the teams themselves. One team only will be selected to give the review, but all will have to prepare it, just in case they are asked!
Key Points	Towards the end of each lesson and at the end of each topic, focus the attention of the class on the key points. Use active learning techniques. For example, invite each team to determine what they think have been, say, the four key points of a lesson. Then reveal your answers (dramatically). Identify the best team solution and let them all reflect on the differences and similarities between theirs and yours.
Rough Paper or Book	Give these to the teams to prepare their responses to questions or problems and to make notes in readiness for their pair or team discussion. See under **Silence**.

Peer Coaching	When there are some issues or points that need understanding get the teams to tackle them through peer coaching. Define as accurately as you can the standard required and challenge each team to bring all its members up to that standard by mutual help. Invite them to indicate when they think they have reached the standard.
Team Teaching	For the purpose of an introductory exposition combine two classes and share the exposition with a colleague. Later invite your teams to try to identify differences in subject interest between the two teachers. (See below under **Disagreement**)
Student Questions	Student questions are more important than teachers' questions. So train them to ask good questions. They need time to formulate them (see **Silence** and **Rough Paper**). When each student has a question they could work in pairs to try to answer each other's question. Teams could subsequently decide and report the most interesting question that has been raised within the team.
Disagreement	Always emphasise that disagreement is interesting, and not an excuse for quarrelling. So when a problem is being discussed by a team, set them the task to define clearly the differences between their individual perceptions. When they have done that then they can report their preferred solution.
Silence	Frequently insist on silence so that everyone can quietly reflect. It gives students the opportunity to complete notes, look back over the work, prepare questions, etc.
Testing	Finish a lesson with a short test on the material covered in the lesson. As this will be for reinforcement rather than permanent assessment, make it into a team competition. No mutual help allowed, but the results are team totals, not individual.
Circle	This device does not use the team organisation. Clear the middle of the room so that all the students can sit in one big circle. A very friendly arrangement, and excellent for general discussion and evaluation at the end of a topic.
Breaks	Don't be afraid of giving breaks, especially during long and difficult sessions.
Snapshot	When you see students performing particularly well, ask them to freeze, look round and take note of the characteristics and quality of what they are doing.
Sweep	This develops from the **Circle**, but on this occasion when one student finishes their response to a question, the person on their right takes a turn, until everyone has had the opportunity to speak.
Whip	This procedure is the same as the **Sweep,** except that now students are asked to respond in one word or one sentence.

'1–10' Line-Up   Students are asked to line up along a continuum from 1 (e.g. 'I really liked what we did') to 10 (e.g. 'It was horrific'). Students are then asked at random why they placed themselves where they did.

These last four techniques are taken from he Critical Skills Programme.

These techniques are designed to make class teaching more interactive. Obviously the list could be expanded a great deal, but ideas for this list should be kept to those that allow paired or team activity for very short periods of time within a lesson that is controlled by the teacher. The more sustained group activities should be kept for a separate list.

Conclusion

This has been an important chapter because it is about the link between a teacher-dominated classroom and a student-centred one. Getting students to learn to respond as a team to small problems and issues is the first step towards independent work and ultimate autonomy as learners. Operating in this way, classroom life becomes much more friendly.

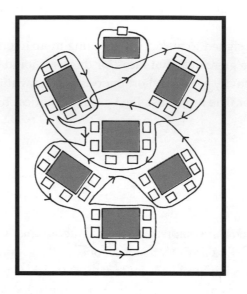

Towards Independent Learning

> ➡ collecting and organizing resources
>
> ➡ the steps towards independent learning
>
> ➡ supervised study

Most of us share a vision of the truly autonomous learner – a person who is highly motivated, thoroughly organised, and capable of making rational and responsible decisions about the use of resources, people and facilities for learning. Such a person would possess what Guy Claxton refers to as the 3R's: 'resilience, resourcefulness and reflectiveness' (Guy Claxton, *Wise Up: The Challenge of Lifelong Learning*, Bloomsbury, 1999).

Most of us also recognise that our students aren't like that! So we think of our work as giving them a progressive training towards the ultimate goal of autonomy. But we have to start where our students are now.

This chapter identifies the steps by which this progressive training might be given. The steps are described in a logical order, but it is not necessary to adhere strictly to that order. Training of this kind is opportunist; the skilled teacher will adapt to the students and to the topics being studied. But always, this will be training on the job. The students will learn how to learn by being involved in real learning tasks. The demands which are made on their maturity and responsibility will grow as they become more capable.

Collecting and organising the learning resources

In respect of classroom management it is possible to identify some important principles. Here they are set out as firm statements with a brief justification for each.

Don't assume that independent learning requires especially designed resources

This is not to deny that more and better resources can considerably enhance the quality of the students' experiences in school. But teachers would be mistaken if they believed that no progress can be made towards independent learning without new resources being bought or locally produced. The best advice to those about to embark on independent learning programmes is to start with the resources that you are already familiar with, and only think about expanding them when the system is running well.

Provide a good coursebook for the student working independently

A student who is asked to work independently even for short periods will benefit from a good coursebook. Such a book would be concise, well-structured, comprehensive and reliable. It would provide the student with a secure framework – a prop in the absence of the teacher.

Put the student in contact with a wide variety of enrichment resources

It is quite wrong to force the independent learner into a narrow `programmed learning' mode in which all stimulus comes from the one package, however carefully it has been designed. Independent work is linked closely with the intelligent use of libraries and other information sources. It is in the application of this principle that the teacher will be able to provide students with the opportunity to develop their Key Skills

Help the student with good assignment material

This is guidance which may have been prepared by the teacher in writing or on tape. It helps with information about resources, and with guidance on strategies and presentation. Sometimes short assignments will take the form of worksheets or task cards.

Prefer resources that are available in small format

Within a classroom where independent learning is being developed the small topic booklet, the single sheet of data, the single illustration, the short audio-tape or video come into their own. They are an economical use of resources and can be sharply focused on the learning tasks.

Normally prefer to buy or borrow resources rather than to make them

Making resources can be so time-consuming, and even with the improved technology available in school, it is likely to compare poorly with what the commercial publisher can produce. The usual exceptions to this general principle are assignments, local material, and material for which there is absolutely nothing available commercially.

Consider small sets of resources, rather than class sets

Class sets are sometimes required, but only where an item is likely to be in constant use by the whole class. For individual and small group work, small sets work better and it is a much more economical system of buying. *Effective Learning Activities* by Chris Dickinson (Network Educational Press, 1997) explores how activities can be designed to make use of small sets of resources.

Always explore the vast resources which exist outside the classroom and outside the school

Quite apart from the quantity and the quality of what is available, there is an invaluable experience for the students in finding and using such resources.

Be systematic in the storage of the resources

Resources are there to be used, and within the classroom a student must be able to find what is required. Elaborate classification and retrieval systems may not be the best solution. Regard the building up of a good resources base as a longterm commitment.

The steps towards independent learning

Resources by themselves do not produce independent learning. We need to look at what actually happens in the classroom. In making progress towards independent learning there are three variables to consider:

- ➡ the grouping in which the students work (individual, pair or small group)
- ➡ the way in which they are prepared and briefed for tasks
- ➡ The ways in which the teacher controls and monitors their progress

The table shows four possible steps by which a teacher might set a class on the road to greater independence and responsibility. As you can see, the teacher starts with the whole class active learning which was described in the last chapter and then adjusts the variables to give the students greater responsibility.

The remainder of this chapter will be devoted to Step 2: supervised study. Steps 3 and 4 will be be tackled in the two following chapters.

Step	Student Group	Briefing for Task	Monitoring and Control
1 Active learning	Team	Whole class	Teacher directing whole class
2 Supervised study	Individual or paired	Whole class	Teacher circulating
3 Supported independent work	Individual paired or small group	Tutorial group	Tutorials and teacher circulating
4 Self-managing Teams	Individual, paired or small group	Negotiation with tutorial group	Mainly by tutorials

The next step: supervised study

A well-known scenario

Supervised study is widely practised. Most teachers will recognise this scenario: the teacher has recognised that young students do not thrive if they have to sit still and listen to expositions all day long. Furthermore, she has also recognised that there are limits to their attention span within a class dialogue. The need to give them something to do is obvious.

So, arising out of the work that has been done so far, the teacher sets a task or a series of tasks to be done individually or in pairs. The explanation of what to do and how is given to the class as a whole. For the most part the teacher makes the decisions, but this need not be so, and the teacher's ideas are often supplemented by suggestions from the students.

The individuals or pairs then proceed with their tasks, and the teacher's role is moving round the class, checking that everyone is on task, helping with problems, making suggestions, giving advice, and at the same time generally supervising work and conduct.

This simple system is widely practised in our schools. It has a number of strengths. It helps the students to be more active and it could be the start of a strong move towards real independence for learners. Students generally like it and the teacher finds opportunity to talk to individuals or small groups – a welcome change from addressing the whole class.

But there is a weakness if the system is allowed to become exclusive: students are for the most part working individually, and they could be deprived of the stimulus of working with others. There is also an important danger: the system could easily become stuck at this point, with the learners still dependent on the teacher's directions. Although they may be active they are not really involved in much decision-making. So we need to examine this system critically, to find out what are the factors that prevent it developing.

The most common cause of the supervised study system getting stuck is, paradoxically, the teacher's own desire to be helpful to the students. We naturally want to feel that we are doing some good and so we are quick to respond to each and every request for help and advice as it comes. Without realising it, we are sending messages to our students that asking the teacher for help is what we expect. Then the pressure of requests builds up and we find the system is quite exhausting, but we justify the expenditure of our effort on the grounds of 'the changing role of the teacher'. In extreme cases this state of affairs reaches a point where the teacher is working harder than any other person in the room, and:

- ➡ has no time of his/her own because all the time is taken up by matters of importance to individual students

- ➡ is under such pressure that answers to questions are given hurriedly and briefly, and sustained dialogue is discouraged

- ➡ begins to lose track of what is happening generally

- ➡ starts neglecting some of the important things like student assessment and evaluation

Some teachers, on reaching this point, abandon the system altogether, saying that it doesn't work. And who can blame them! On the other hand it might be better to tackle this 'mother hen syndrome' head on.

Overcoming the weaknesses

In order to do this we may, at least at the beginning, have to suppress some of our instincts! We must recognise that bustling activity by the teacher is not a reliable indicator of student learning. In fact, there is likely to be more hope in the very opposite, where the teacher is not under pressure and has some discretionary time available.

Let us work on this concept of discretionary time. Let us assume that if the teacher has more discretionary time during a lesson, it will be possible to use that time to better effect. And it will also mean that the students are beginning to take on greater responsibility.

If we accept this assumption, we are left with the inescapable conclusion that we need to reduce the number of student questions! At first this may seem an outrageous idea, and it clearly needs justifying. But if we analyse the questions that the students ask, we begin to see possibilities, because the questions we need to cut out are the unnecessary ones! And there are often plenty of those. But we must approach this with sensitivity and offer stimulating and acceptable alternatives. Consider these ideas as ways of doing just that.

Make sure that the initial briefing for a task has been thorough

Has this been given enough time? Has it been explained in sufficient detail? Have students been asked to summarise the main points to show that they have understood? Has time been given for questions about uncertainties or possible problems? The objective of each briefing must be for students go away absolutely clear about what they have to do, where the resources are to be obtained, how they might set about it, and what the finished presentation should look like. In the early stages of the progression towards autonomy there is nothing wrong in being prescriptive. For many students, the first need is to learn how to deliver the right work at the right time. Of course, no briefing, however skilful, will eliminate all the possible questions; but it will succeed in cutting out the unnecessary.

Make sure that the students can cope with the resources which have been prescribed for the task

Is the reading level right? Has provision been made for those who have difficulty in reading? Are there any possible sources of confusion about sequencing within the resources? Are the written assignments (if any) crystal clear? This question of differentiation is a major one: clearly, if students are unable to understand some aspect of the text, activity or task, then interruptions will proliferate. Behaviour also is likely to deteriorate, and the teacher's discretionary time will have gone.

Make sure that the teacher will not be burdened with questions about location of resources or equipment

This may mean delegating some tasks to students. It may also mean investing some time early on in making sure that all students understand where resources are kept and what are the rules for acquiring them.

Encourage the students to seek help from each other before approaching the teacher

This should certainly be encouraged, even demanded. If students are organised in teams, as in the cabaret layout, they will already be accustomed to doing this. Whenever a student approaches the teacher with a question, it should be assumed that this is only after support has been sought from within the team.

Make explicit arrangements in advance to cope with possible recurring crises

Try to anticipate what these crises are likely to be and make some arrangements so that they are dealt with by the system, rather than by ad hoc effort on the teacher's part. Take, for example, the students who work fast and regularly finish a task before the majority: Why not provide for them a box of particularly appealing additional tasks (rewards)?

Analyse the questions that are received from the students which a view to improving the system

Over time this really pays off. For each question, consider why it was asked. Was it caused by poor briefing, by inadequate resources, by poor support within the team, or is it just a problem which could easily occur again?

Of course, even if these suggestions are enthusiastically put into practice, they won't entirely eliminate the questions. But that is not the aim, which is, rather, to reduce the number of questions. For the most part it will be the trivial, the obvious and the easy that are eliminated, leaving the teacher free to concentrate on some of the heavier problems.

Building on strengths

So where does this leave the teacher who has successfully cut out most of the student questions which are simple or trivial or unnecessary? Well, that teacher now enjoys some discretionary time and can now seriously consider setting up meaningful dialogues with the students. How might this time be used to best effect? Consider the following:.

Spend more time listening to individual students

Encourage them to expand on their difficulties and their problems. It not only makes them feel better, but it gives them practice in talking about their work, and it helps the teacher diagnose what the underlying problem might be.

Don't answer a student's question directly

Try to get the student to answer the question, or get another student to join in the discussion. Certainly don't answer the question hurriedly or abruptly. Gentle prompting, paraphrasing, and redefining the question will all help.

Intervene more

Don't just hang about waiting for their questions. Try a little skilful intervention. Ask some questions of your own. The aim is to find out how well they are understanding and seeing all the implications. Give a little time to explaining or illustrating the ideas.

Form groups

Not permanent groups, but little ad hoc groups. It is a friendly way of intervening and students enjoy it. They gain confidence in a small group, and the experience helps their motivation.

Don't keep reverting to class teaching

There is a temptation, whenever a student raises a problem that seems significant, to explain it to the whole class. It seems an economical way of doing things. In fact, it is counterproductive. It breaks students' concentration, and when they are left to pick up the threads of their work they can feel frustrated. It is nearly always better to tackle the problem with the small groups described above.

Keep a low profile

Do what you want to do quietly and unobtrusively. If you give an impression of bustle and noise, the students will do the same.

Conclusion

The supervised study system can represent a good first step for students who are being trained to accept greater responsibility for their own learning. Coupled with the active learning techniques described earlier, it can add up to a stimulating repertoire.

The system reveals all its potential when the teacher has the confidence to let students get on with their work without intervening, and when the students are happy and competent to solve their problems without making excessive demands on the teacher, as most teachers who use this system have found to a greater or lesser degree. The greeting to a visitor to the classroom is often: don't worry about the students – they can get on by themselves for a bit. The build-up of responsibility is clearly taking place, and there is potential for progress into new territory. But everything hinges on the amount of the teacher's discretionary time.

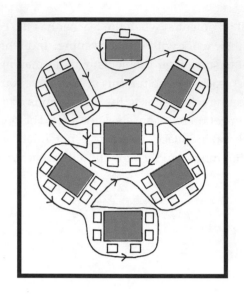

The Independent Learner and the Group Tutorial

➡ the 'golden scenario'

➡ the group tutorial

➡ the group tutorial and independent learning

➡ the tutorial in its own right

In the last chapter we examined how a teacher might improve the monitoring and support of independent learners. We suggested that in order to do this the teacher had to gain more discretionary time. The only way to do this was to cut out unnecessary and trivial demands that the students might make.

Both teacher and students would gain. The teacher would not be under such pressure and would be able to devote time to students in more meaningful ways. There would be more listening, more genuine dialogue, more student participation. The teacher would give greater attention to the briefing of students, to the resources they were using in their tasks, and to the possibilities of support that students could give each other.

These are substantial benefits in their own right, and a classroom managed in this way would offer stimulating and satisfying experience for the students. But the most significant thing about this classroom is that there now exists within it a growth point of great potential. We refer to the possibilities for the small group tutorial, led by the teacher. The purpose of this chapter is to explore these exciting possibilities.

The golden scenario

We have described how a supervised study system can be improved in order to make the interaction between teacher and students much more meaningful. By devoting just a little more time to each encounter the teacher is able to learn more about the student, get the student to contribute more, and to raise the level of the student's thinking and commitment.

This kind of high quality support works particularly well when small ad hoc groups are formed for a few minutes. It gives a sense of collaborative working. Students prompt and help each other, or even vie with each other; they are spared the psychological pressure of being the sole of focus of the teacher's attention; they share a sense of achievement and often make commitments to go on sharing or supporting. When the encounter is finished the students disperse and resume their individual or paired work. The experience has been an enjoyable interlude within the normal routine. Do the students lose the personal touch through being grouped in this way? It may happen sometimes, but the more likely outcome is that they get a strong feeling of belonging which is very powerful.

There is also the benefit that the teacher's time is being used economically. Instead of working stolidly round 30 individual students, the teacher may accomplish just as much in four or five encounters with small ad hoc groups.

This is the golden scenario. It is the starting position from which most good systems of independent learning grow. It would be a mistake, however, to rush on. There is a lot to be said for spending time improving and refining the supervised study system. Students need to be trained to work effectively in this way. Here are some suggestions for improvement and consolidation, which should help provide a firm base for the next advance.

➡ Frequently discuss the system with the students: they must understand what your objectives are.

➡ Praise all examples of enterprise and responsibility.

➡ Take every opportunity to teach them about their own thought processes. You need to add to their vocabulary: analysis, conjecture, hypothesis, evidence, and so on. Praise the thoughtful response, especially one that is (usefully) wrong.

➡ Constantly emphasise their independence. Praise the student who perseveres and tries to get solutions.

➡ Monitor carefully your own use of time. Have you succeeded in increasing the amount of your discretionary time? Try to increase it without abandoning your reasonable level of support for the students.

The group tutorial

When students are working well under the supervised study system described in the last chapter, the teacher may feel that they are capable of advancing still further down the road towards autonomy. The way ahead is through the group tutorial. Consider this assertion and this problem:

The assertion   The small group tutorial holds out more promise of raising educational standards than any other single strategy. Within the small group the teacher can offer tailor-made support and guidance, and can raise the intellectual level of the experience quite dramatically. Within the small group each individual student feels a stronger sense of personal worth and responsibility.

The problem   How can we run these small-group tutorials when class sizes are so large and syllabus pressures so demanding?

The assertion is a bold one, but more and more teachers now support it, and a substantial number are proving that the problem can be overcome. If so, we live in exciting times.

The vision of a group tutorial

Let us pretend that the problem (the class and the pressure of syllabus) doesn't exist. Let us try to describe how we would like to organise the learning of a small group of students, using all the advantages of small numbers and applying our best thinking about teaching and learning skills. This should give us a vision of our ultimate goal. We know that, in practice, we are unlikely to realise it quickly, and we shall never realise it entirely, but at least we have something to aim for. As soon as we have described the vision we shall start looking at ways of making progress towards it.

An overview of the group tutorial

The group tutorial is an opportunity to provide an intensive educational experience. It penetrates deeply into educational objectives. In the small group the teacher can tune in accurately to students' existing knowledge and readiness and help them to raise their intellectual level. The small group lets the teacher demonstrate the personal worth of each individual, and encourage each one to contribute. It enables students to support each other and use each other as resources in natural, conversational ways. It lets us recognise:

➡ the 'ideas' people who introduce novel and creative solutions

➡ the 'process' people who encourage the group to keep trying

➡ the 'product' people who want to get finished

➡ the 'people' people who keep the others happy

So we can develop a collaborative working group that makes use of individual members strengths.

The atmosphere of the small group can so easily become calm, positive and friendly, yet disciplined and purposeful. Students get a sense of their own worth and are eager to take on responsibility. The occasion has a feeling of privacy; students are not afraid to confess ignorance or confusion, or to ask for help. Throughout, the teacher is able to become a good role model of the mature learner – intellectually honest, respectful of others' contributions, disciplined in the pursuit of agreed objectives, rigorous in evaluation. And there are countless opportunities to teach the skills of working as a member of a group, of finding out and studying, reporting and presenting.

The structure and processes of the group tutorial

The size of the group
An optimum size is probably about five, although successful tutorials can be conducted with any group in the range from four to eight. Outside this range, problems increase rapidly. As the group gets smaller, the variety of contribution is diminished and the tutorial may begin to lack vitality. As the group gets bigger, it becomes increasingly difficult to keep all students equally involved, and to allow sufficient time for each individual.

There is also a limit on the number of tutorial groups that one teacher can successfully manage within a single class. It is wise to keep the number below six. So for a class of 30 students it might be best to organise five tutorial groups of six students each.

The composition of the group
A good mixture of abilities and personalities often makes the most interesting tutorial group. So normally a group would include both boys and girls, and should cover a fairly wide band of ability in the subject. It is unwise to attempt to organise tutorial groups by strict ability streaming; the weakest group presents too many problems. On

the other hand, many teachers find that small groups spanning the whole ability range are difficult to manage. Some experimentation is worthwhile, bearing in mind the subject matter and the characteristics of the students. There is certainly no universal solution to this problem.

The lifespan of the tutorial group

We should certainly aim for the benefits of some continuity, so the group should have a reasonable lifespan. But there are good arguments for not making an arrangement permanent. An occasional change during a year gives students an opportunity to establish new relationships and have a sense of a fresh start. It gives the teacher the opportunity to reorganise in order to fit the needs of a new component into a programme of study.

The frequency and length of tutorials

The choice is clearly between longer tutorials held only occasionally, and shorter ones held very frequently. The former arrangement tends to suit the more mature and experienced students; the latter the younger and less experienced. The range of possibilities is very wide. At one extreme a good Year 12 group might pursue a topic through independent study with a weekly tutorial lasting an hour. At the other extreme a teacher working with a large lower Year 8 class may feel that each group should have perhaps two or three very short tutorials during an hour-long period; the size of the tasks set would be also very small.

The agenda of the tutorial

Tutorials can have many different aims, so it follows that they must have different agendas. No two tutorials are likely to be the same. It all depends on the needs of the learning situation. Here is a list of possible agendas:

(a) the briefing tutorial. This is required at the beginning of a new topic or at a significant point in the development of the topic. The purpose is to make sure that the students have thought through all the implications of the work that they are going to do independently. They will need help in:

- ➡ clarifying the objectives of the work

- ➡ exploring the resources available, making judgements about the contribution that each resource might make, looking at the strengths and weaknesses of each item to be used

- ➡ devising a strategy for tackling the work: the sequence of activities, the relative importance to be attached to different components, the difficulties and problems which might be encountered, opportunities for extending the work if time allows

- ➡ agreeing the nature of the finished product : in what form will it appear, how big will it be, when exactly is it due?

The briefing tutorial is probably the most common type of tutorial and probably the most important. Setting students complex independent learning assignments without proper briefing is the surest recipe for failure.

(b) the review tutorial. This agenda is also frequently used. The students have completed a learning assignment, and the purpose of the tutorial is to review and assess their work. Some possible components are set out below:

➡ the student's own report on the work – what has been done, what has not been done, what has proved difficult, what has proved particularly interesting, what implications are there for the work as a whole

➡ a comparison of the approach adopted by different students with reflection on the significance of the differences

➡ an assessment of each student's work (it being assumed that the teacher has had the opportunity to look at the work before the tutorial), done publicly with the active involvement of all the group

➡ the recording of achievement and targets for future work on a record or profile sheet. This will usually be a formative document, but if the tutorial is at the end of a piece of coursework or module, then the records might be summative

This review tutorial provides an excellent way for teachers to manage the Assessment for Learning strand of the National Strategy for Key Stage 3.

(c) the discussion tutorial. This is required if a topic requires the students to reflect and consider different interpretations of facts. A well-structured discussion enables students to try out the ideas and engage in critical debate about them.

(d) the coaching tutorial. This is an occasion where the teacher reverts to teaching in a more traditional sense. It is needed where there are particularly difficult concepts and ideas to be mastered. The small group provides the best environment for the analysis of ideas and diagnosis of problems. The weak student gets the best possible support here because of the feedback which the skilful teacher is constantly seeking.

(e) the planning tutorial Similar to the briefing tutorial, but the purpose may be to look further ahead and take a wider view than just the next piece of work. This sort of tutorial might be conducted when students are about to embark on major coursework projects.

(f) the managerial tutorial. Sometimes the group needs a simple business meeting to get a lot of arrangements sorted out. This is a valuable experience, especially when it is conducted in a businesslike and disciplined way.

(g) mixed agenda. Often a tutorial has a specific purpose and the agenda is designed accordingly. But there are also more general tutorials. In these the characteristics of more than one of the main types described above are combined. For example, a tutorial may start with a review of work completed and then go on to plan the next piece of work. Or it may carry out a small piece of planning and then spend the rest of the time on discussion of some of the more important issues.

Whatever the needs, the agenda of the tutorial must be explicit. Students must know what the purposes are, and they must be encouraged to learn to work to an agenda.

Educational objectives

The tutorial can also be described in terms of educational objectives – in other words, asking the question 'What differences are we trying to bring about in our students?' There are four categories to be considered:

➡ **The intellectual**. We are trying to encourage students to use their thinking skills, not merely learn things by rote. A skilful tutor is constantly finding ways of getting students to express themselves clearly and become more aware of their own thought processes. It is all about structuring, analysing, evaluating, and using high-level vocabulary.

➡ **The personal**. Within a small group the individual counts for more. A good tutorial demonstrates concern for individual well-being and personal development, over and above the needs of the task in hand. The atmosphere is warm and supportive; this builds self-esteem and respect for others. Learning takes on a new personal meaning.

➡ **The social**. Within the small group the relationship between the members is a powerful contributor to success. Students learn to cooperate, to use each other as sounding boards and as sources of knowledge and inspiration. They learn to compete and challenge and argue a case, but without losing their mutual respect (or their tempers!)

➡ **The managerial**. The tutorial group is also a disciplined, task-oriented group. There is frequent reference to objectives and standards and deadlines. A crisp, business-like style helps ensure that the group has a constant feeling of progress and achievement.

Of course this is ambitious. High achievement in these four areas demands skill, particularly in achieving a balancing between them. Sometimes the different objectives seem mutually exclusive. It is easy to see, for example, that a tutorial may become so task-oriented that it partly inhibits the development of the personal objectives. The important point is that the tutorial is small enough to enable the teacher to adjust in sensitive ways. And this is one of the aspects of tutoring which is so intriguing.

Styles and techniques

The styles and techniques used in a tutorial reflect closely the educational objectives. The style is best summarised by a quotation:

Achieving flexibility by empowering people

1. Involve everyone in everything.
2. Use self-managing teams.
3. Listen, celebrate, recognise.

(Tom Peters, *Thriving on Chaos*, Pan, London, 1988)

The teacher who is new to tutoring could not do better than to use this short quotation as a personal check-list for self-evaluation.

Towards the group tutorial

Most teachers will find themselves in sympathy with the vision of the group tutorial as described. They will also experience a sense of frustration that the conditions under which they work do not seem to encourage progress in that direction.

Progress seems to be easiest in Years 12 and 13 where numbers are often small, the students are more mature and sometimes highly intelligent, and there is a tradition of private unsupervised study. The problem is at its worst in the large classes of the lower school, where the students are younger, of mixed ability, and there is a need for them to be supervised at all times. We shall concentrate our thinking at the lower school end!

How can we extend the small group tutorial within the confines of the lower school classroom? The answer is, with difficulty and slowly! Yet it is amazing what can be achieved. The following suggestions should help.

Improve the golden scenario

Our golden scenario was the improved supervised study system. The key was that the teacher gained more discretionary time so that encounters with students could become more meaningful and less hasty and abrupt. It is worth working at this over a period of time. The simple indicator of success is longer intervals between requests for help initiated by the students. When five minutes go by with the students all busy on tasks, the teacher can begin to feel that real progress is being made. It is a question partly of encouraging students to be independent and to support each other, partly of ensuring that briefing, resources, and housekeeping have all been attended to. (The last chapter explained these ideas in more detail.) It is only when the supervised study system is working really well that the class is ready to make the move towards the tutorial system.

Seize opportunities to work with groups rather than individuals

Whenever it makes sense to do so, respond to an individual's question by involving a group of students. You might already have the class working in active learning teams and it would make sense to use such a ready-made group. But it is easy to involve a small number of students. Make it into a little ad hoc tutorial. Get the members to try to answer the question. Point out some of the interesting implications. Take the opportunity to check their understanding of the task and the subject matter. And leave it at that! It should only take a minute or two, and you can then get back to overall supervision of the whole class. But the students are beginning to learn to operate as a team.

Team-build

We have already discussed the importance and the possibilities of team-building. It needs doing for the tutorial groups from the very beginning. The more they are proud of their membership and have a feeling of solidarity with each other, the more effective the tutorials can be.

Make plans for the transition between whole class work and work which is driven by tutorial

It simply is not possible to leap from whole class teaching into tutorial-led work in one move. What is the rest of the class doing while you are briefing the first tutorial group? And the second tutorial group?

The transition must be made through the supervised study system. Set a common task by whole class briefing. When you are satisfied that it is going well and you have sufficient discretionary time, start giving each tutorial group in turn a short briefing for a short task.

Use mini-tutorials

In the early stages, when students are still relatively inexperienced, these tasks and briefing sessions should be very short indeed. We want to try to get the system rolling without risking major disaster. These mini-tutorials are an excellent way of getting the students accustomed to the cycle and aware of the fact that the review of their work will be thorough.

Clearly there are some big compromises here. You are unlikely to achieve the vision of a group tutorial that we have painted in this chapter. But in a progressive training towards independence, mini-tutorials like this are an important step in the right direction.

Leave time to reflect and evaluate

It is wise to leave a little time for reflection and evaluation. So after a few lessons experimenting with the mini-tutorial it is be useful to consider the strengths and weaknesses of what has been achieved so far. Improvements for the next round could be considered. It is always worthwhile seeking the opinions and advice of the students. If they feel part of an interesting development they will not only be helpful in thinking through the issues, but will also work better in class (at least in the short term, which is a bonus in the early stages!).

The group tutorial and independent learning

An important relationship

In our overview of classroom we listed some of the common forms of independent learning activities. The relationship between these activities and the group tutorial needs to be carefully considered.

The diagram below looks deceptively simple:

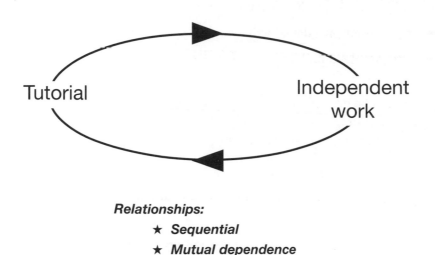

Relationships:
- ★ *Sequential*
- ★ *Mutual dependence*

The arrows might at first seem to show just a sequence of activities: a tutorial is followed by a period of independent learning, which is in turn followed by a tutorial, and so on. This is perfectly true. But the arrows also demonstrate mutual dependence. Independent learning depends on a high quality tutorial. But also, use of the tutorial depends on the students' ability to work independently. The two are inextricably linked. And for the teacher who is trying to establish independent learning, this is a typical 'chicken and egg' situation. There can be no progress on one side without equivalent progress on the other.

So the good tutorial helps students to plan and prepare effectively for their independent work, but also provides a forum for their reporting and reflecting. It has a businesslike aim, but is also an opportunity for discussion and a meeting of minds. We can illustrate this in practice by reference to a common type of independent learning.

Project work: an illustration

Project work is increasingly required or offered as part of the course for external examinations. The aim is to broaden students' educational experience and to give them opportunities for independent work.

Although a student may choose a personal topic and will be assessed individually, there is still a strong case for tutorial support to be arranged in small groups. This is much better than forcing the student into isolation for this work. The student can gain experience and intellectual stimulation from membership of a group, and the simple sharing of ideas and approaches can be valuable.

The first briefing
The purpose of the first tutorial must be to carry out initial planning. The student should be asked to come prepared with details of his/her interpretation of what has to be done, and in turn should speak about:

➡ the objectives of the project

➡ the limits of the project (what should be included or left out)

- the resources likely to be required
- what the end-product will be (to be described in detail)
- a proposed calendar of activities
- any perceived problems

There should be brief discussion by all the members of each project and the students should be encouraged to make notes as to what has to be done immediately in order to get the work plan into a satisfactory shape.

Subsequent tutorials

These could be used in a variety of ways. Here are three possibilities:

- The group works as a whole, listening to interim reports given by individual members – asking questions, making suggestions, and offering opinion about what has been done so far.

- The group works as a whole, discussing strategies and tactics for the learning tasks that are being undertaken. This is an opportunity for sharing ideas and information about resources.

- The members of the group work on their own tasks, but the tutor withdraws individuals for intensive tutorial support.

Whatever the style used, the students must learn to make notes during the tutorial and to regard their notes as a form of contract between them and the tutor. Many teachers have designed their own contract forms to help students use a structured approach.

Between tutorials

Students are likely to require help between tutorials. But the teacher should aim to cut this to a minimum:

- concentrate on high quality briefing at the tutorial
- encourage students to plan their contribution to the tutorial so as to cover all the points there and then.

Of course, this is a counsel of perfection. But it is worth some effort to try to stop project work becoming an excessive burden for all.

The tutorial in its own right

The tutorial is an educational experience in its own right. It is important to say this because it has sometimes been assumed that the tutorial is purely a support arrangement for independent work. This implies that it is only when working independently that the student's responsibility is being developed.

It is important to express the opposite view. Consider our own responsibilities as members of a profession. Does our responsibility manifest itself when we are allowed the privilege of working quietly on our own? Or is it more apparent when we have to work with other people – planning, justifying, negotiating, explaining, requesting, reporting, questioning? These are surely the real indicators of responsibility. And it is in the small group tutorial that the student begins to learn these skills about adult life.

The teacher's role is crucial

Working as a member of a small group is a sophisticated adult activity. Our students need their teacher in this situation more than they need anything else. It is the teacher who sets the standards and the style and provides the role model. This in no way contradicts the student-centred philosophy that guides the system.

So it is vital that the students should experience the well-conducted, teacher-led tutorial before being asked to embark on group activities in which they are entirely self-managing. This latter is the ultimate objective, but we are taking a step-by-step approach. Our next chapter considers these possibilities.

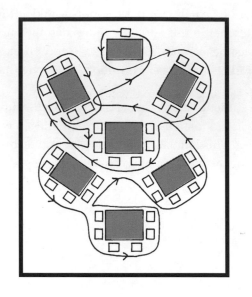

The Self-Managing Team

- ➡ the case for the self-managing team
- ➡ purposes and functions of the self-managing team
- ➡ criteria for the formation of self-managing teams
- ➡ occasions for self-managing teams
- ➡ techniques and processes for self-managing teams

This chapter takes our learners a further step forward on the road towards autonomy. It explores the possibilities of much greater freedom and discretion for the learner.

The idea of the self-managing team is an attractive one, highly regarded in the adult world as a better way of enabling people to give their best and get a high level of satisfaction from their work. The basic principle is that the team decides how best to tackle a job, allocating responsibilities and tasks to members. So individual work is not at all excluded.

The question for teachers is whether this way of working can be used with young students in school. The answer depends, of course, on their state of readiness. If they have grown accustomed to taking on greater responsibility through active assignments and group tutorials, then it is likely that they could begin to make progress on the lines suggested in this chapter. Certainly all students should have had some experience of the self-managing team by the time they reach the age of 16. It seems reasonable to suppose that it should be part of the regular experience of students in the 16–19 age range. However, as in all classroom management, it is wise to proceed with caution and not to build up expectations too rapidly.

The case for the self-managing team

The case for the self-managing team rests mainly on its potential for increasing the motivation of its members. These are the features by which it provides motivation:

- ➡ members of the team make their own decisions as to how the work is to be tackled

- ➡ the teacher provides an information and ideas service which is designed to help teams develop their own thinking

- ➡ the teacher offers support to the team, which generates self-confidence and ambition without undermining its autonomy

- ➡ the teacher acts as a sounding board for the team's ideas and plans

- ➡ the teacher acts as a coach, training members in the roles, responsibilities and techniques of the self-managing team

When these features are present the team members begin to get a sense of ownership about the work and a strong desire to succeed. They begin to support each other and to seek assistance from each other. They begin to know the deep satisfaction which comes from working as a member of an effective and respected group. They look upon the teacher as a consultant. In this sort of atmosphere, knowledge and understanding grow.

A word of caution is necessary. These features of the self-managing team cannot be put in place instantly. They are the result of progressive training towards autonomy, and almost invariably a development from some of the systems and techniques described earlier.

It is not possible to generalise as to when students are ready for the self-managing team. Some 11-year-olds will work well in self-managing teams; some 17-year-olds may be completely disorientated. The technique is to introduce the idea slowly and on a small scale. This gives the teacher an opportunity to identify needs and respond to them; and it gives the students time to adjust to the new demands that are being made on them.

Coaching in the roles, responsibilities and techniques should have started during teacher-led tutorials.

The purposes and functions of the self-managing team

The underlying purpose is to increase the opportunities for student–student interaction. When they are accustomed to talking to each other about their work, in the absence of the teacher, the prospects for their learning are very good indeed. Each individual student begins at his/her own starting point.

Within any team there are bound to be differences in knowledge, experience, and attitudes, but each student will influence the direction in which team thinking develops – setting the pace, asking questions, formulating answers, criticising the direction of the argument. Through this process students are helped to assume responsibility for learning, and develop a sense of ownership of new knowledge and understanding. Knowledge becomes personal knowledge, through the learner's participation and commitment.

But it is inevitably a slow process. The students may not always achieve the conclusions and vocabulary that the teacher would like. The temptation is to intervene too frequently, to get them on the right track. But this would be an unfortunate judgement. The students need time to express themselves in their own way, to explore ideas, to use their imagination, to share in the formulation of ideas and solutions to problems, and to plan and organise the work of the group. This is not to imply that the teacher should totally abdicate during periods of team activity. Preparation, follow-up, and timely intervention are all vital. It all depends on some very fine judgements on the part of the teacher.

Criteria for the formation of self-managing teams

Group size and composition

These questions have already been discussed in the chapters on teams in active learning and teacher-led tutorials. Similar principles should apply here. In fact, it is very likely that it will be the same group that will operate in different modes according to different needs:

- as a team within an active class teaching lesson
- as a tutorial group for supporting independent learning
- as an occasional self-managing team

But we have also made the point that these teams should not be regarded as permanent. There is a lot to commend the idea of using a team for a particular job in a programme of study, with the assumption that it will be disbanded when the job has been done. This arrangement gives students a wider experience and helps sharpen the focus on specific objectives and the need to be business-like.

Leadership

If the teacher is not going to lead the group the question of leadership needs to be addressed. In many adult groups of five or six participants the group can often be leaderless because the members are sufficiently skilled to handle any tendency to dominate or disrupt. This is a lot to ask of young students. So it is better to nominate a leader. This decision could be made by the teacher, but it is better to encourage the group to choose its own leader for a particular purpose. This means that the role would be a temporary one and leadership would therefore come from different members at different times and for different purposes. It would help if, when a new task is being considered, the teacher invited each team to choose a new leader. In this way most of the group members would get a chance, if they so wished.

The teacher's coaching of the self-managing team could usefully concentrate on the guidance and support of the leader. Quite young students can learn how to apply simple rules of procedure, how to move the discussion along by asking stimulating and exploratory questions, how to keep reminding the team of its goals, how to summarise in order to help everyone's understanding.

However, there may well be groups and situations where the teacher feels that the team can operate without a nominated leader. This is stimulating and well worth trying, particularly in the 16 to 19 age range.

Individual responsibilities

In addition to the elected leader it may be useful to encourage teams to give specific jobs to the individual members. The team could agree a short job description for each job (helped by a model which the teacher has provided). The jobs can be rotated. Typical jobs might be: timekeeper, secretary, process observer, resources manager. Ideally everyone in the team should have a job.

Occasions for self-managing teams

Where do the self-managing teams meet?

In an ideal world each team would have its own home-base. Conditions are unlikely to permit this, and many teachers might be cautious about such an arrangement. But the alternative of keeping all the groups in the same classroom presents difficulties of space and disturbance. Compromises are worth investigating. For example, an adjacent storeroom or even the corridor outside might offer space for one group, which would relieve the pressure. At all times the teacher is trying to push forward the frontiers of independence. An important principle is to give a group more responsibility just before the members seem ready for it.

When do the best opportunities occur for self-managing teams?

Logically this kind of group work should come at a fairly late stage in the study of a particular topic. In the early stages the students will have had the need for general orientation and stimulus and motivation, and this can best be provided by the teacher. Then there is a stage at which more information is accumulated, ideas developed, observations and experiences enlarged, and this can often be done by individual working. Group work comes most appropriately when the individual members of the group are ready. This state of readiness is reached when one or more of the following has happened:

- ➡ students have spent some time working on their own, finding out information, developing ideas or practising skills

- ➡ students have received a common stimulus during which there has been no opportunity for them to react, other than privately, e.g. viewing a video or working on a computer

- ➡ students have shared a common experience where there has been much opportunity for individual observation and personal reflection, e.g. an educational visit

- ➡ students are known to have had some personal experiences in their out-of-school lives which will have some bearing on the work.

The message is that there can be no worthwhile group work until the individual members can bring to the group their individual and different knowledge, observations, experiences, perceptions and attitudes. And they must have had time to acquire all this.

What are the typical occasions?

These are very similar to the occasions when the team is set small assignments in the whole class active learning system. The important difference is in the scale of the assignment and its duration. In the self-managing team there is a much bigger assumption made about the organising capabilities of the team.

Some of the suggestions made here could form the nucleus of a personal checklist. Eventually the repertoire available to a subject department could be very large, and individual teachers would benefit by knowing which colleagues had already had some experience of a particular technique.

1. Experts

Challenge each group to become as expert as they can on one particular aspect of a topic. The topic would probably have to be negotiated so that unnecessary overlapping was prevented. Give them plenty of time to prepare and lots of advice and help with resources and general organisation. Then each group in turn becomes an expert panel, either making a presentation to the whole class, or responding to questions.

2. Mastery learning

For the topic being studied define as accurately as you can the standard expected of every student. Give the teams a good idea of the kind of test which will be used. Challenge each team to bring all its members up to a standard within a limited time. Encourage mutual aid.

3. Pass the problem

Invite each team to prepare a problem for consideration by another team. Advise them that the problem must be a big one which will require an extended answer. They must avoid simple questions of fact. So they will probably include questions starting with Why...? or How...? When the problems have been prepared they are passed on to another team. Each team is then given time to work on the problem it has been given before being asked to make a statement giving its considered response.

4. Twenty questions

This is a much shorter exercise but it can be effective if teams are allowed time to work out their strategies. First, each team chooses an animal, vegetable or mineral from the topic being studied. Another team is then allowed 20 questions to discover what the object is, but only through questions that can be answered by YES or NO. Encourage debate within the questioning group to try to determine the best strategy.

5. Delegated tasks

Invite the team to approach a topic or project by delegating work to its individual members. Each team member is allocated part of the topic and at the end of an agreed time is expected to: (a) provide a set of notes to summarise the main points, (b) present questions or problems for the team to discuss, and (c) provide test questions for the individual team members.

6. Games and simulations

Where these are available the self-managing team is the ideal way of using them. At their best they can contribute a great deal to the educational development of the students taking part. There are likely to be gains in communication skills, in general motivation, in knowledge acquisition, in creativity, and in interpersonal skills.The demands on the students are considerable and advice and support are crucial.

7. Structured discussion

Invite the team to explore a whole topic through discussion. Start them off with an agenda but leave plenty of space for their own directions. Give them lots of help in matters of timing and procedures.

Techniques and processes for self-managing teams

The typical occasions described above represent a formidable challenge to any group of young students. Even if they have been well grounded in more active ways of learning and have had experience of well-conducted tutorials they will still not find life easy in the self-managing team. So they need some high quality advice and support.

There may be a temptation to put them through an intensive training in the techniques and processes before asking them to work as members of a team. Undoubtedly something can be achieved in this way, but these skills, like most skills, are best acquired on the job. So the teacher needs to have a repertoire of advice and training up the sleeve ready to be used whenever the students seem to be ready and in need of it.

So the suggestions made here should not be delivered to the students as a course. Instead they should be used as brief interludes during the work, giving the students the opportunity to reflect on the processes which are at work and how they might make more effective use of their own and their fellow students' talents.

House rules

Some simple house rules will be useful. They need to be specially designed for each class, bearing in mind age, experience, special subject requirements, and competence in self-management. The following suggestions give an indication of the kind of rules that may be helpful.

- ➡ On each occasion the leader will decide, after consultation with team members, exactly what the agenda is to be, and the scribe will write it down where everyone can see it.

- ➡ Members of the team speak only when invited to do so by the leader.

- ➡ The leader is responsible for making sure that the discussion and the action are fairly shared among the team members.

- ➡ At the end of each session the scribe will write down what has been agreed and check that everyone has accepted it. If action by team members is called for then it needs to be recorded what is to be done, by whom and when by.

After having received a basic framework of rules, members of the team should be invited formally to adopt them and then occasionally to add rules of their own in order to make their collaboration even more effective.

Thinking skills

Teams need help in setting about their tasks in an intelligent manner. It is wrong to assume that they can operate in a sophisticated way without some training. Young students can learn better thinking strategies. The best way is to give them some simple models to use. These will serve as props to help them set about their deliberations in a structured manner. When they find these successful they will be eager to build on them.

Show them how to look at a question systematically. Ready-made mini-agendas have proved very helpful. For example:

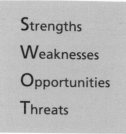

Strengths

Weaknesses

Opportunities

Threats

When faced with an issue to be discussed the team may use the SWOT technique as a ready made mini-agenda. All members will first concentrate on the strengths of the argument or arrangement; then they will examine its weaknesses, and so on.The technique helps to make sure that the students look at every side of a question and do not leap to instant conclusions based on the first most persuasive argument they hear.

Here are other examples of mini-agendas.

The ADD technique:

Advantages

Disadvantages

Discussion points

Factors

Factors affecting oneself

Factors affecting other people

Factors affecting society

Factors to be ignored

Timescales

Long term

Medium term

Short term

Teams should be encouraged to develop their own mini-agendas as procedures for tackling problems.

Train them to see a problem from the opposite point of view

This should not be done casually or lightly. Encourage them to develop the opposite view in a full-blooded way, using some of the mini-agendas. In this way they will learn to get a much better understanding of the strengths and weaknesses of an argument.

Train them in the development of alternative solutions

The principles are the same. Rather than leaping into advocacy of an attractive solution, they should spend time working out the detail of the alternatives, even if, at the end, they will come to reject them. They need to have it explained to them that original thinking often starts by trying to justify what seems unjustifiable.

Group skills

The members of a team also need help in recognising the processes which are at work within the group.

- What proportion of the talk does each member have?

- What roles are the various members playing? Initiator? Leader? Co-ordinator? Agitator? Scapegoat? Builder?

- What kinds of contributions to the discussion are being made?

  - *questions*, asking for information, help, opinion?

  - *answers*, offering suggestions, opinion, information?

  - *comments* that are supportive, friendly and understanding?

  - *remarks* that are hostile, tense and disagreeing?

If the team has appointed a process consultant, that student should be invited periodically to report on the effectiveness of the group as a unit. Discussion should follow and the leader should aim to get clear understanding and commitment so that the team can operate more effectively in the future.

Summary

The skills of working with people are a subject in their own right. It is worth finding out what is happening in the school generally to encourage students to think on these lines. Often there is valuable work going on within a pastoral tutorial or Personal and Social Education programme, which should be transferred into the other subjects of the curriculum.

Interpersonal Relations

- ➡ background
- ➡ classroom strategies
- ➡ classroom tactics
- ➡ the disruptive student

Expanding the repertoire of teaching and learning seems fine, but teachers are often anxious that the greater complexity of classroom life may lead to bigger problems in maintaining a smooth working atmosphere. The classroom could so easily become a haven for laziness and disinclination and a hiding place for disruption and malice.

The truth of the matter is probably that the broad repertoire classroom has a much greater range of possibilities With careless handling the worst could happen and standards of behaviour and attitude would deteriorate. On the other hand, the student-centred approaches do improve motivation, and when working in small groups or as individuals, students do develop different relationships with their fellows and with their teacher.

So we ought to lean towards optimism. If we can manage interpersonal relations with skill, we can achieve a much more positive atmosphere, leading to more effective learning. So this must be given high priority. It is an ever present need. Most teachers acquire their skills in this aspect of management through experience and intuition. However, it is hoped that the analysis in this chapter will help to heighten awareness and reinforce some of the best techniques.

The background

There has always been a steady flow of publicity which claims that standards of discipline in schools have declined. There is no shortage of evidence: aggressive and disruptive behaviour, acts of violence against persons and property, use of alcohol, drug abuse, defiance of authority.

It is true that many teachers have to spend a disproportionate amount of their time dealing with disruptive students and the consequences of their actions. They could also add to the list of evidence many other manifestations which do not make the headlines, but which do make the teacher's work much more difficult: boredom, unwillingness to cooperate, anxiety, indifferent health, and other symptoms of underlying distress.

There are some who, in the face of the all these problems, have abandoned educational objectives in favour of counselling and crisis management. They argue that it is impossible to teach these students anything until their personal lives have been sorted out. The trouble is that this is never achieved. There are others who declare themselves to be teachers, not social workers, hoping that the problems will go away, or that somebody else will deal with them. There is a third group, and they are probably the majority, who are desperately torn between the two points of view outlined above. They appreciate that students do not live their lives in compartments, and that success can only occur across a wide front embracing every aspect of a student's life and development. The solutions are not easy.

This is the not the place to attempt a detailed analysis of the causes of the problems. However, a summary of factors is given below without any attempt to elaborate.

Society as a whole

- ➡ It is now recognised that 'a job for life' is no longer to be expected. Today's school student can expect to have several jobs during his or her working life, with a consequent reduction in security.

- ➡ Today's organisations are bigger, and seem to offer less scope for individuality.

- ➡ Globalisation has resulted in the loss of the UK's industrial economic base. The replacement of heavy industry by a service economy has resulted in males losing their traditional role and not yet finding a new one.

- ➡ There has been increased use of violence by small groups in order to attain political or personal gain.

- ➡ The decay of inner city areas has proceeded faster than measures to combat it.

- ➡ Unfair discrimination is still a feature of our society.

The home

- ➡ physical neglect – meals, clothing, health

- ➡ mental neglect – absence of conversation (language deprivation), contempt for anything intellectual, determined exclusion of rationality as a basis for decision-making

- ➡ emotional neglect – depravity in the home, emotional cruelty, mental abnormality in the home, lack of love

The school

- ➡ impersonal and insensitive regime

- ➡ focus exclusively on academic achievement

- ➡ excessive use of regulation, creating an impression of distrust

- ➡ lack of respect for the opinions or feelings of students

Adolescence

- ➡ tensions resulting from physical changes

- ➡ the drive towards independence, which is not always consistent and smooth

- ➡ youth subculture and the power of peer pressure

With all this to contend with, it seems a miracle that so many of our adolescents are good students with a strong sense of their responsibilities and opportunities. We need to do everything in our power to help them.

Success in building good personal relations within the classroom depends on both long-term strategies and short-term tactics.

Classroom strategies

What is it that marks out the successful and respected teacher whose students seem naturally to work with positive and constructive attitudes? What advice might such a teacher give to a beginner?

Get the 'knowledge'

Like the London taxi driver who needs to know the detail of the city, the teacher needs to develop a deep understanding of the students' environment. This means knowing about the catchment area of the school, knowing about students and their families, knowing about students' outside interests, knowing about their other activities within the school, knowing about the school – its traditions, its rules and its events. Encyclopaedic knowledge of this kind is vital. It is what distinguishes the established teacher from the newcomer (however senior). A wise teacher builds that knowledge continually.

Prepare thoroughly

Prepare teaching thoroughly – materials, activities, assessments. When students know that the teacher is filling time, or having to change activities because materials cannot be found, or is unprepared for problems which emerge, then respect and confidence ebb away.

Prepare administrative matters thoroughly. Keep on top of routine. Nothing undermines a student's confidence more than a flustered teacher.

Build an image

Students tune in to the image which the teacher presents to them from the very first appearance. Subconsciously they are watching and recording every initiative, every reaction, every expression of feeling. It all builds up into an image.

The knowledge already discussed is an important aspect of the image. Students need to feel that the teacher knows about them, their families, and their home area. They must also get the impression that the teacher knows the school systems and procedures thoroughly. For a newcomer it is worthwhile deliberately setting out to demonstrate early mastery in order to make the point to students. A little name-dropping or a little demonstration of inside information can help!

Then create a serious impression of purpose. Trying to seek quick and easy popularity through ingratiating practices or being 'with it' can be counterproductive. The old, cynical advice 'Don't smile until Christmas' has some force. Students come to like their teachers first by respecting them and then happily discovering that they are also very human. The serious and firm impression of purpose is conveyed by being thorough in one's own contributions and in demands made on the students. This means attention to detail, and an assumption that students will take their work seriously and with a sense of responsibility.

There needs also to be an impression of strength and resolution. While your normal stance will be calm and pleasant, students should soon discover how you react in a crisis. The newcomer needs to demonstrate fairly early that he/she will not flinch from responsibilities and will be contemptuous of any attempt to start negotiations following a flagrant breach of rules or instructions.

But this needs to be balanced by the impression of a caring adult. Every opportunity should be taken, and often outside the classroom, of establishing some personal contact with as many individual students as possible. Discovery of a shared interest, a word of praise after an achievement, a word of sympathy after a disappointment, a little practical help or advice, an appreciative word to a parent (who is sure to pass it on), can all help to establish a bond. Most teachers can recall instances of relationships much improved by taking part in some informal activity such as camping, expeditions, social work, and sporting activities.

Classroom tactics

Longterm strategies can help a teacher build up good standards of personal relationships which result in good discipline. Nevertheless, teachers are dealing with young people who may not be capable of coping with all the stresses of their lives and who often react with laziness, insubordination, defiance, mischief, aggression or destructiveness. It is a pity if these behaviours are allowed to undermine the development of good classroom practice which is designed to help students learn effectively and take on greater responsibility. We need to examine now the classroom tactics which will help to avoid or prevent these troubles, or, if they do occur, help to handle them in the most effective way.

Unfortunately, advice about tactics is less reliable than advice about general strategies. The complexity of classroom life is responsible for this: it is multidimensional, with many different kinds of activities, many different purposes, and many people having different needs and different styles. Things happen simultaneously. There is an air of immediacy about the place. At any one time the teacher is considering what to do next, thinking ahead about the development of the lesson, watching students' progress, looking out for anything that might disrupt the smooth flow of the work. And then there are the unpredictables, such as interruptions from outside, the unforeseen difficulties, the minor accidents. In this sort of context the teacher's action and reaction are driven more by intuition than deliberate, reflective thinking about alternative courses of action.

Another factor that makes advice about classroom tactics unreliable is the fact that different teachers use apparently contradictory tactics with equal success! So these suggestions are offered tentatively, recognising that they may be based on experience that does not match the experience of others. We hope simply that some of them prove useful to some teachers!

Design and establish good starting routines for lessons

➡ Make sure that the room and resources are in a state of readiness.

➡ Arrive before the students, if you can.

➡ Teach students what is expected of them on arrival. For class teaching the permanent instruction might be: 'Collect a copy of each item laid out on the resources table near the door. Have your rough book open and ready.' For independent or group work the instructions might be: 'Collect the materials you are currently using and resume work.' At the beginning of the lesson the teacher's role should be purely supervisory, and students should be instructed to defer any individual approach to the teacher, except in emergency. A clear signal should be agreed which marks the end of this brief but vital period. During this supervision the teacher controls as much as possible by the eyes. Avoid speaking if possible; use the eyes and a few hand gestures.

Establish a clear understanding about 'speaking' rules

➡ There must be a clear signal that the teacher wishes to speak to the whole class. And that signal must mean three things: 'stop talking; put down any materials or equipment; and listen'. Always use the same words as the signal. Make an issue of it whenever the signal is ignored. The younger secondary students enjoy practising these little routines, and they become conditioned to them. If you are trying to introduce the idea to older students it is more difficult. But quiet persistence pays off.

➡ During class teaching, whether in the form of class dialogue or in active learning, there needs to be clear understanding about the procedure for a student to speak. Simply to allow anyone to shout out contributions soon leads to chaos, and it is a poor training in responsible discussion. In class dialogue the old-fashioned hands up procedure works well enough. In active learning, organised in teams, the use of a spokesperson for a team is strongly recommended.

Develop clear routines for accomplishing regular organisational tasks

These include taking the roll (if this is required), distributing materials in class teaching, clearing away at the end of lessons, forming groups, using apparatus. The way ahead in this is to make a mental note every time a small amount of chaos occurs. Consider what little routine might help to stop that occurring again.

Adopt a purely supervisory role at regular intervals throughout a lesson

We have already examined this as an important component in the supervised study system. But the teacher is really supervising all the time! The danger in supervised study is to become too absorbed in helping a small group, so that standards in the class generally begin to slip. Short supervisory stints can help – a quick scan of the whole room with a brief intervention wherever it might seem necessary.

All control actions should be as unobtrusive as possible

➡ Some teachers can wither with a glance. It is worth being able to do it! All gestures and signals can be effective: a finger to the lips, a hand signal to sit down, a finger to beckon, a nod of approval to allow something to happen, a shake of the head to say no, a shake of the head to signal disapproval, an arm akimbo to signal patience getting low. It can all be done without saying a word!

➡ If it really is necessary to speak to a student, approach them and speak quietly. The rest of the class is not disturbed, and if it is a reprimand the student does not lose face and will accept it without wanting to retaliate.

➡ If the general level of noise tends to escalate (and it usually does) check it early on and unobtrusively. 'Shsh!' can work wonders. A quiet teacher makes a quiet class.

Continue to demonstrate your knowledge

➡ Always use a student's name.

➡ Make every encounter have at least one small personal touch in it.

Maintain the momentum and smoothness of the lesson

➡ Keep up the pace.

➡ Don't be long-winded.

➡ Don't go on about inadequacies or misbehaviour.

➡ Don't over-elaborate an anecdote. Don't overteach the obvious.

➡ Don't interrupt the whole class during independent work with instructions or exhortations. Don't keep chopping and changing.

Anticipate discipline problems and act quickly and decisively

➡ Alertness, anticipation, quick recognition, prompt but unobtrusive action are the characteristics of the good disciplinarian. Where the teacher is uncertain (and this is common) it is best to approach a student in a non-critical way, asking the student to report what progress has been made or what problems have been encountered. This will get him or her back on task without the need for unsafe accusations.

➡ If the misbehaviour is overt it is best to remove the student from any possible audience. Set them to work in a different part of the room, making it clear that they can return to base when the particular task is completed. This helps the student to accept the arrangement.

Avoid confrontation

➡ Confrontation is public and emotionally charged. It can result in frightful escalation and unwillingness to back down on either side. It is usually watched with fascination by the rest of the class.

➡ An openly defiant student should be removed from the classroom. It is to be hoped that most schools have arrangements for this to be done with supervision. The teacher can then deal with the problem privately and (probably by then) more calmly.

The disruptive student

In our imperfect world many classes contain one or two students who are constantly disruptive. They may exhibit a combination of these symptoms: unable to concentrate or persevere; noisy; physically restless; inclined to interfere with other students; quarrelsome; react emotionally if reprimanded; easily bored; easily defeated by difficulties; often believe they are being victimised; often want to be friendly to the teacher but seem unable to prevent themselves being cheeky or silly.

For many such students a major problem is low self-esteem. Effective differentiation and regular small group tutorials will help some of them. But there may be a number of hard core students for whom little works; they can do a lot of harm in a classroom.

The teacher is often forced to spend a disproportionate amount of time with them, and confrontation occurs, which brings an abrupt halt to the work of the whole class. How can one allocate time and effort? On the one hand, there is the programme of study and the needs of a whole class of students; on the other hand, the disruptive student clearly needs some special attention. Quite clearly, outside help may be required and may be available. But meanwhile the teacher needs to develop a strategy for the problem.

The lesson-by-lesson handling of the disruptive student needs to be guided by the general tactics already discussed, but in a systematic and deliberate way. The idea of teaching good behaviour, known as behaviour modification, has gained some acceptance. The argument is simply that the teacher does not have the time or resources to tackle the underlying causes, but can at least concentrate on trying to teach good behaviour. The system relies heavily on systematic reinforcement – mainly rewards for good behaviour. Because the causes of the disruptive behaviour are mainly beyond the reach of reason, the modification takes place through experience rather than through reasoned argument.

A programme for a disruptive student might be developed on these lines:

1 Find out what rewards might be valued by the student. These will vary according to age and interests – praise, privileges, reports, material rewards, tokens.

2 Make specific agreements about behaviour over short periods of time, with a clear understanding about the rewards.

3 Do a formal check and, if the standard has been reached, make the award.

4 Try to arrange that tasks that the student prefers and finds pleasing follow tasks which are not preferred. The pleasant tasks are then seen as a reward for the completion of the unpleasant.

5   Try to enlist the support of team members. If the reward is for the team, then it is likely that the student will get a lot of help and encouragement.

6   Use negative reinforcement sparingly. Public reprimands will be counterproductive.

7   Give attention to the student when behaviour is good; withhold it when it is bad.

This is a counsel of perfection, but it is important to have it always in mind, because the instinctive reaction is to do the exact opposite. Remember that the disruptive student wants attention. So spend more time reviewing good work and behaviour, in a more public way and with a show of friendship. Always deal with bad work and bad behaviour privately, briefly, and without too much fuss.

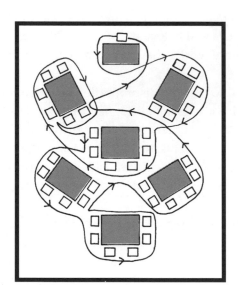

Classroom Management

The Improvement of Classroom Management

➡ setting up an evaluation programme

➡ a framework policy for teaching and learning

   - outline model
   - detailed model

➡ setting your own policy for teaching

➡ evaluating existing practice

➡ mutual observation

We have argued that teaching is a complex business, and that is the justification for the concept of classroom management. So we have to accept that improvement of such a complex business requires deliberate and purposeful action. It will not happen by wishing, or by occasional drives. It needs to be planned as a long-term, regular, sustained programme of activities which become part of the teacher's way of life.

It is best if this can be arranged on a team basis because the benefits of shared thinking, group planning, mutual aid and mutual criticism are substantial. Ideally the team should be a real team within the school organisation: for example, a secondary school faculty or department. But much can also be accomplished by a small ad hoc team set up informally. A partnership of two or three teachers who have similar responsibilities and who share a commitment to the improvement of their teaching, will accomplish a lot. Likewise, a small cluster group of teachers from neighbouring schools can become a significant force for improvement. To work entirely alone must be regarded as the last resort, but it is better to do that than to drift into complacent defeatism.

Setting up an evaluation programme

Establishing the group

In an ideal world the team would be an existing team within a school. The idea of setting up a programme for the improvement of teaching would spring naturally out of a debate which is a normal part of the team's processes. There might be some dissatisfactions with present practice. There might be a perceived opportunity springing from consideration of the key action points following an Ofsted inspection.

The part played by the leader of the team in the early stages will be a critical factor. It may be necessary to extend awareness among the team members and to build up interest and commitment. In some teams the proposed programme might appear as a threat, and this needs to be handled with great care. Ultimately team members are going to have to adopt an approach which is rigorous and self-critical and which is capable of listening to criticism made by others. Time needs to be given to such anxieties; they cannot just be brushed aside. Much should be done by example rather than by exhortation. The support and advice of people outside the team should be sought, but with a sensitive appreciation of the extent to which this might increase the sense of threat among the team members.

Team members should be able to determine their own contribution to the programme. Some may be eager to get thoroughly involved in all the programme activities, but others, for one reason or another, may prefer a more limited role. The latter group may well lack confidence, but if their mode of contribution is accepted and valued they will still be part of the team, and able to extend their activities at a later date without having to do a U-turn.

Time and effort given to team-building will pay off. The programme should not proceed until everyone in the team is committed to it, even if the commitment is very small-scale.

Devising a policy for good teaching and learning

The team cannot make any progress until there is some kind of agreement about the aims and objectives of the programme. If we are setting out to improve the quality of teaching we need to get agreement about what constitutes good teaching. But is it not a fact that teaching styles differ, and who is to say that one style is better than another?

The problem seems to be an intractable one. Yet we can be much more optimistic than appears possible at first. To begin with, a debate about what constitutes good teaching is a desirable thing in its own right. We ought not to evade it simply because it might reveal different perceptions. Second, when teachers get down to detail there is often more agreement than an early general discussion might have suggested. Third, the production of a policy for teaching can be a quicker exercise than many people initially expect. So the message must be to get started.

The ideal policy has these characteristics:

➡ it enjoys the commitment of all the members of a team of teachers

➡ it is based on systematic study of relevant guidelines

➡ it responds to local conditions, policies and developments

➡ it has been produced as a team effort

The policy should always be regarded as provisional. This partly explains why a team can produce one quickly. It is provisional and will be brought up to date and improved regularly in the light of experience. In no sense is it a once-and-for-all, state-of-the-art tablet of stone! There are bound to be new influences, new pressures, new ideas. And there are bound to be second thoughts based on experience of using the policy.

The policy should occupy pride of place in the team's documentation. It should be displayed prominently, shown to visitors, given to newcomers. It should have a place on the agendas of the team's regular meetings. So what might such a policy look like? A model is outlined opposite.

A policy for teaching and learning: a model framework

An outline model

The first step is to determine the main headings under which we might describe teaching objectives within the team. This will give us a framework for the detail of the policy. In discussion to determine these headings we shall need to bear two principles in mind:

➡ The headings must provide a comprehensive coverage so that all the objectives and associated activities can be included within the statement of the policy.

➡ The headings should not overlap each other. This is easy to say and almost impossible to achieve entirely. But it needs attention so that the worst overlaps are avoided.

When the headings have been determined, then each should be defined by a short statement of the general aim. Based on the ideas developed in this book, an example of a framework for a policy of teaching now follows. Note that the general aim which follows each heading is expressed as an assertion.

1. **The classroom**
   The classroom is attractive in appearance, and functional.

2. **Planning and preparation**
   There is evidence of sound planning, based on appropriate guidelines. This is backed by detailed and thorough preparation.

3. **Learning resources**
   The classroom has resources of sufficient quantity, quality, and variety in order to give maximum support to the teaching programme.

4. **The teacher as leader and presenter**
   The teacher demonstrates personal attributes, technical competencies, and subject knowledge that will promote the students' learning in an atmosphere of respect and confidence.

5. **The students as active and independent learners**
   The students take an active part in the lessons and demonstrate their developing independence and sense of responsibility.

6. **The classroom social system**
   The students have the opportunity to work as members of small groups, in pairs, and individually.

7. **The intellectual climate**
   The teacher constantly raises the intellectual level of the verbal exchanges which take place in the classroom.

8. **The interpersonal climate**
   The teacher and the students enjoy each other's company, are mutually supportive, and treat each other with courtesy and respect.

> ### 9. *Management and control*
> The teacher operates an efficient system of management and control. This rests on firm arrangements and on appropriate procedures.
>
> ### 10. *Management of time*
> The teacher and the students get the most out of the time available through a well-developed sense of priorities and a sense of economy in the expenditure of time.

These headings need to be thoroughly discussed before proceeding further. Clearly, individual teams will have their own different ideas as to how their work can best be classified, but it is hoped that the examples given above will serve as a model, and for many will also serve as a basis for a framework, requiring only a few modifications.

The detailed model

Armed with a set of headings and general aims, we are now ready to fill in the detail. The recommended method is to take each heading in turn and ask the simple question: What would an observer actually see in the classroom to suggest that the broad aim is being achieved? In other words, we are looking for indicators. We can express these best as assertions, in the same style as the general aims except that these will be much more detailed and specific. Our indicators should be, as far as possible, both observable and incontrovertible. But inevitably value judgements will have to be involved. Teaching does not lend itself to simple, mechanistic assessment.

The headings of our model are now repeated with suggested indicators appended.

1. The classroom

The classroom is attractive in appearance, and functional.

1 The room is clean and tidy, occupied only by equipment and materials in current use.

2 Wall displays are attractively arranged and are relevant to the current teaching and learning.

3 Relevant reading and reference material is available to students at all times, without the need to request it.

4 The layout of furniture gives students as much workspace as possible, and allows for flexibility between individual work, small group work and class teaching.

5 There is an adequate supply of all the writing and drawing materials and equipment that the students are likely to require.

6 The resources for learning currently in use are stored in such a way as to permit quick retrieval.

7 Adequate equipment is available to permit the projection of slides and filmstrips, and the playback of audio-tapes.

8 When required there is access to TV, tape recorder and CD player, OHP and computer facilities.

9 There are clear policies, rules, and procedures relating to the shared use of the room and its facilities by students when teaching is not taking place.

2. Planning and preparation

There is evidence of sound planning based on appropriate guidelines. This is backed by detail and thorough preparation.

1. There is clear statement about the place of the programme of learning within the guidelines of the National Curriculum.

2. More detailed educational objectives have been derived from the statement of broad aims laid down by the programme of study.

3. There is a detailed summary of the content of the programme.

4. There is a description of the kinds of learning activities which are intended for each stage in the programme.

5. Explicit arrangements have been made for the evaluation of the programme.

6. Appropriate learning resources have been carefully assembled and organised.

7. Some guidance material (e.g. written or taped assignments, study guides) has been prepared in advance.

8. Documents have been prepared to assist the teacher in classroom management (e.g. a teacher's guide, a desk plan).

9. Appropriate tests have been written or acquired.

10. There is good stock of teacher presentation materials (e.g. audio visual aids, copies of handouts).

3. Learning resources

The classroom has resources of sufficient quantity, quality, and variety in order to give maximum support to the teaching programme.

1   Resources are differentiated to match the needs of individual students (particularly with regard to reading levels of printed materials).

2   Quantities of resource items have been determined by the needs of the programme (eg class sets; small sets; individual copies).

3   Printed resources have design appeal, in addition to providing the necessary date and stimuli.

4   Resources are classified and stored in a way that helps the students use and find them.

5   Resources are diverse, so that students can learn through visual and aural experiences as well as reading alone.

6   There are, as appropriate, specimens, models, artefacts, etc.

7   There are explicit arrangements for the students to use the central library/resources provision in the school.

8   Contacts with any local providers of resources have been made.

9   The teacher has access to sources of information which will support the work.

10 Students display a high level of competence in the handling and use of resources.

4. The teacher as leader and presenter

The teacher demonstrates personal attributes, technical competencies, and subject knowledge that will promote the students' learning in an atmosphere of respect and confidence.

1   The teacher's manner is normally patient and good-humoured.

2   The teacher creates a constant impression of self-confidence and self-control.

3   The teacher shows flexibility and an ability to respond creatively to events.

4   The teacher's instructions, descriptions and explanations are brief and clear.

5   As a result of the teacher's skills as discussion leader, the students demonstrate a high level of participation.

6   The teacher uses effective questioning in order to raise the level of students' thinking.

7   The teacher's voice is used in varied, interesting, and encouraging ways.

8   The language used by the teacher is carefully measured for its accuracy and for its appropriateness.

9   The teacher demonstrates a sound knowledge of the subject matter.

10   The teacher draws on a large repertoire of example, illustration, anecdote, and vivid detail.

5. The students as active and independent learners

The students take an active part in the lessons and demonstrate their developing independence and sense of responsibility.

1   When students arrive at the beginning of the lesson they take active steps to prepare for work.

2   Students display initiative in finding the resources and equipment they need.

3   Students display initiative in getting help with difficulties before seeking help from the teacher.

4   Students take an active part in discussion in a measured and responsible way.

5   Students frequently offer help to fellow students.

6   Students are often organised in teams as a way of supporting their active and independent learning.

7   Students frequently follow up classroom work with further investigation in the school library or elsewhere.

8   The teacher is able frequently to step back from the action because the students are all so involved and absorbed.

9   The teacher gives time to training the students in the skills of personal organisation and in the skills of learning.

10 Students accept substantial responsibility for the various housekeeping tasks of the classroom.

6. The classroom social system

The students have the opportunity to work as members of small groups, in pairs, and individually.

1   Students experience a balance of teaching and learning activities, organised as a whole class, in small groups, in pairs, and as individuals.

2   Within the groups there is a strong sense of mutual support.

3   The teacher gives time to training the students in the skills of small group work.

4   Group size is small enough to ensure participation of all members, yet large enough to produce diversity of response.

5   The composition of the groups has taken into account ties of friendship and the need to produce diversity of style.

6   There is a wide range of tasks for performance in groups: problem solving; games and simulations; discussions.

7   The teacher has given the group adequate guidance on the procedures and standards for group work.

8   All group work is conducted in a disciplined manner.

9   There are well-organised opportunities for groups to report the outcomes of their work.

10   Students demonstrate their developing skills in group work by respecting the views of others and by engaging in debate without quarrelling.

7. The intellectual climate

The teacher constantly raises the intellectual level of the verbal exchanges which take place in the classroom

1   The teacher allows time for students to express their ideas and to expand on them.

2   The teacher sets a good example of higher levels of thought.

3   The teacher encourages those who attempt to express themselves in abstract terms.

4   The teacher phrased questions in ways which will provoke divergent responses from students.

5   The teacher uses, and encourages the students to use, language in a caring and measured way, appropriate to the needs of the situation.

6   The students demonstrate a willingness to analyse knowledge and ideas.

7   The students demonstrate a capacity for developing and testing hypotheses in a thoughtful way.

8   The students are ready to criticise information and ideas in a constructive manner.

9   The students are not afraid to express value judgements and to have them discussed.

10 The students constantly seek to structure their knowledge and understanding in meaningful ways.

8. The interpersonal climate

The teacher and the students enjoy each other's company, are mutually supportive, and treat each other with courtesy and respect.

1   The teacher shows a personal interest in individual students for their own sake, beyond the needs of the immediate learning task.

2   The teacher actively fosters a sense of group cohesion in work and in discipline.

3   The teacher is courteous towards individual students.

4   The teacher makes frequent use of praise and encouragement, but in a measured and sensitive way.

5   The teacher frequently accepts a student's expression of feeling about the work or the organisation.

6   The teacher frequently accepts or uses ideas expressed by a student.

7   The students display their willingness to work co-operatively.

8   The students feel free to signal their difficulties and to alert the teacher to organisational mistakes and problems.

9   The teacher and students occasionally share their sense of humour.

10   Students sometimes disagree with the teacher in a mature and non-threatening manner.

9. Management and control

The teacher operates an efficient system of management and control. This rests on firm arrangements and on appropriate procedures.

1   The teacher has established procedures for monitoring each student's work.

2   The teacher has established clear personal objectives and commitments for each student.

3   There is an efficient system for the continuous recording of each student's tasks, progress and achievements.

4   Feedback is given to the student in order that the student can build up knowledge about his/her own performance.

5   The teacher gives clear directions on task procedures and encourages students to understand the structure of the lesson and of the course.

6   Students are encouraged to help in decision-making about the organisation of the work.

7   The teacher handles minor lapses in students' behaviour in a competent way, demonstrating alertness, sure judgement, and confidence.

8   The teacher copes with the complexities of classroom life in a calm and confident way.

9   The smooth flow of classroom activities is maintained by the teacher, particularly when there is a transition from one mode to another.

10 The teacher uses positive reinforcement (praise, incentives, peer manipulation) to overcome problems caused by disruptive students.

10. The management of time

The teacher and the students get the most out of the time available through a well-developed sense of priorities and a sense of economy in the expenditure of time

1 The teacher succeeds in allocating a high proportion of the available time to academic work.

2 The students spend a high proportion of their time engaged on their learning tasks.

3 The students experience a high degree of success during their engaged time.

4 The teacher maintains a good balance in the use of time on supervisory, organisational, and teaching tasks.

5 A high proportion of the teacher's time is spent in 'substantive interaction' with the students (i.e. explaining, questioning, describing, illustrating).

6 The teacher has eliminated unnecessary routines and activities from his/her own performance.

7 The teacher has delegated to students responsibilities and tasks that are within their competence.

8 Simple and speedy procedures have been devised for tackling routine events and recurring problems

9 There is evidence that the teacher plans ahead so that time in lessons is used most effectively.

10 The teacher regularly reviews the conduct of lessons in terms of the effective use of time by both teacher and students.

Setting your own policy for teaching

The example given above of a policy for teaching can be used either as a model to start thinking, or, even more usefully, as the basis for a department's own policy.

We have already claimed that the first provisional policy for teaching could be produced quite quickly, and there is a lot to be said for doing just that. The policy is only an instrument. Although it may start life as less than perfect, it is better than no instrument at all, especially when its use can lead to improvements in its design.

So the suggestion is made that a department should allocate two hours (during an in-service day, for example) with the firm intention of producing a provisional policy for teaching. Here are some suggestions as to how this might be done by a department team.

1. The first task is to establish the framework of headings with their broad statement of aims. In order to do this, each member of the team should have access to the model provided in this chapter.

   ➡ Get each member to work privately for a short time in order to suggest a framework. Many of the headings given in the model may prove acceptable; others will need to be changed.

   ➡ After a brief period for private work go through the model's list of headings, and agree to adopt or reject and replace or modify each in turn.

   ➡ You should aim to have your own list of headings within half an hour. if debate gets too fierce remind members that they are only producing a first draft, not a statement for all time!

2. Then allow members to work in pairs with each pair taking the responsibility for suggesting indicators for one or two headings (depending on your numbers). Suggest that they use the model to provide some of the ideas.

   ➡ Go through the model's list and accept, reject, or modify each indicator. Teachers will almost certainly wish to develop some indicators which more accurately represent the needs and aspirations of the department.

   ➡ They could be advised to do this through an initial brainstorm to provide as big a bank of ideas as possible, leaving the critical analysis of these until later.

3. Use the last half hour to receive and accept or modify the reports from the pairs.

   ➡ Encourage people to be generous and not too fussy (first draft!).

   ➡ Aim to have a document ready for typing by the end of the half hour.

Of course it is too rushed. But isn't all teaching like that? The point is that there is now a tool, however imperfect, waiting to be used. And that is what we must think about now.

Evaluating existing practice

We are now ready to put into practice the cycle of improvement described in the introduction to this book. Here are the steps.

Step 1:
Prepare an evaluation of the teaching as it exists now.

Use the department's policy for teaching as the agenda for a meeting. Try to arrive at some conclusions under each of the headings.

Step 2:
Identify key areas for improvement

This could be done at the same meeting as Step 1, but there could be an advantage in giving time for reflection and devoting more time to Step 2. The size of the key areas is a matter for personal decision. On one occasion a department might decide to cover a number of areas for improvement, accepting that each part could only be given limited attention. On another occasion the department might decide to concentrate a lot of time and effort on one specific aspect of the policy.

Step 3:
Formulate plans for improvement.

The team should decide upon specific objectives for improvement and consider appropriate strategies. This step need not take long, because the indicators already listed in the policy could provide ready-made objectives. But it may be desirable to work out more detail, and to give some idea of the actual location of the improvements within the departments and work, and also some idea of the timescale involved.

Step 4:
Decide how the evaluation will be conducted.

Teachers could certainly report on their conclusions about their own work. But, if it can be arranged, the observation of each other's work can be valuable. We are going to discuss this separately in the next section. Other useful sources of evidence can be from independent observers and from the students themselves.

Mutual observation

This must surely be the most fruitful approach to the improvement of teaching and learning. There is increasing acceptance that the isolation of teachers in the classroom is harmful, both from a personal point of view and from the point of view of the profession as a whole.

Comparisons can be made with other professions, where to observe and to be observed are regarded as an essential part of the initial training and subsequent development of the individual member. Opening up the classroom has become a commonly expressed desire. The initial idea is often little more than a feeling that if teachers could only drift in and out of each other's classrooms, a lot of knowledge about each other's styles an techniques would be picked up, casually and almost accidentally. The idea seems attractive and not potentially threatening.

We need, however, to be much more disciplined and purposeful than this. The use of a policy for teaching is one way of getting started. There are some points to be made.

- ➡ This is observation for mutual support and improvement, not teacher appraisal.

- ➡ All observation should be conducted on a mutual basis and on terms of equality. If a head of department wishes to observe members of the department, the best way to start is to invite them to observe the head of department first.

- ➡ The nature of an observation should always be determined by objectives that have been chosen by the teacher to be observed.

- ➡ Results from an observation are the property of the observed.

- ➡ Observation must always be followed by a discussion between the observer and the observed.

It is worth mentioning briefly that in addition to using a policy for teaching as the basis for mutual observation, a department could decide to use one of the published systems. Many such systems have been devised, mainly by research workers. For example, one of the oldest and best known is the *Flanders Interaction Analysis*. This is valuable where a teacher is engaged in whole class teaching and wishes to test the amount and kinds of student involvement. The system can be used in a very simple way, or it can be more elaborate leading to a very sophisticated analysis of classroom interactions. (Interested teachers should consult Flanders, N., *Analysing Teaching Behaviour*, Addison-Wesley, 1970.) Another valuable source of tools and techniques for mutual observation is the school's induction tutor. During the induction year, newly qualified teachers are expected to be observed formally on six occasions. As a result of this, induction tutors and mentors have often received training in the techniques of classroom observation.

Of course there are difficulties in getting all this into place. The tightness of school timetables does not help. But mutual observation is so important that it should be given priority, perhaps using supply cover for the purpose in preference to using it to send teachers outside to courses.

Some final points

Adopting a systematic approach to the improvement of teaching is not necessarily a sure guarantee of instant success. There may be some failures on the way and some disappointments. A few suggestions may help.

Look wide for support

Working entirely alone can be dispiriting. Making improvements needs helpers – personal counsellors; experts; those who control the money.

Give the programme sustained effort

Don't give up at the first signs of difficulty. Classroom improvements often come about slowly, but they will yield to persistence.

Avoid 'programmitis'

This means getting more interested in the programme than the things that it is supposed to serve. The symptoms are: too many meetings; too much documentation; rigid procedures; the exclusion of any activity which does not fit into the programme

Aim high

It is worth it to go all out to make a real difference. This often means concentrating one's efforts. But when substantial differences are made, morale is given a great boost; and other people take notice. So aim high!

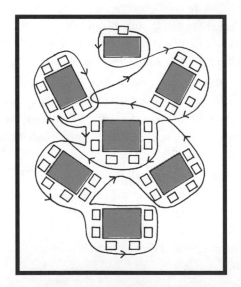

Appendix

Selected List of References

Brighouse T (1990). *What Makes a Good School?* Network Educational Press.

Department of Education and Science (1988). *Secondary Schools: An Appraisal by HMI.* HMSO

Department of Education and Science (1979). *Mixed Ability Work in Comprehensive Schools.* HMSO.

DfEE (1999). Circular 5/99: *The Induction of Newly Qualified Teachers.*

DfEE (2000). *Teacher Effectiveness.* The Hay McBer Report.

The Critical Skills Programme (2001). Network Educational Press Ltd.

Duke D (ed.) (1979). *Classroom Management. The 78th Yearbook of the National Society for the Study of Education.* NSSE.

Dunkin M and Biddle B (1974). *The Study of Teaching.* Holt, Reinehart and Winston.

Gage N (ed.) (1976). *The Psychology of Teaching Methods. The 75th Yearbook of the National Society for the Study of Education.* NSSE.

Hopson B and Scally M (1980). *Lifeskills Teaching.* McGraw Hill.

Lewis R (1986). *The Schools Guide to Open Learning.* NEC

Lincoln P (1987). *The Learning School.* British Library.

Marland M (1981). *Information Skills in the Secondary School Curriculum.* Methuen Educational.

Miller J (1982). *Tutoring: the Guidance and Counselling Role of the Tutor in Vocational Preparation.* FEU.

NEC/NCET (1989). *Implementing Flexible Learning: A Resource Pack for Trainers.*

Ofsted (2000) *Handbook for the Inspection of Secondary Schools.* HMSO.

Reid M, Clunies-Ross L, Goacher B, and Vile C (1981). *Mixed Ability Teaching.* NFER-Nelson.

TVEI (1989). *Developments 10: Flexible Learning.* Training Agency.

US Department of Education (1986). *What Works: Research about Teaching and Learning.* US Department of Education.

Waterhouse P (1988). *Supported Self-Study: An Introduction for Teachers.* NCET.

INDEX

A

Active learning, 43-9, 95
Advance organizer, 22-3, 33-4
Assessment, student, 54, 63
Audio-visual aids 31-2

B

Behaviour modification, 85-6
Briefing, 55, 67-8

C

Class dialogue, 20, 38-41
Cluster groups, 87
Communications, classroom, 97
Consolidation phase, 23, 34
Critical Skills Programme, 13, 40, 45, 49
Cycle of improvement, 15-17

D

Differentiation, 9-10, 55, 85, 93
Discretionary time 54, 56, 59-60
Discusssion techniques, 40-41, 94-6
Disruptive students, 85-6

E

Evaluation, classroom, 14, 66, 87, 102
Experiential learning, 14
Exposition, 33-8

F

Flanders Interaction Analysis, 103
Furniture, classroom, 29

G

Games and simulations, 75, 96
Group skills, 78, 96

I

Independent learning, 17 56, 64, 109
Individual learning, 15, 56, 64, 109
Induction, 12, 103
Interpersonal skills, 81-5

L

Layout, classroom, 25-8
    cabaret style, 27, 43-4
    dining room style, 27
    workstations style, 28
Leadership, 94, 99

M

Management and control, 99

O

Observation, mutual, 102-3
Ofsted, 10, 16, 22, 87

P

Paired work, 21
Peer coaching, 48
Planning, 92
Policy for teaching and learning, 88-90, 101
Project work, 67-8

Q

Questions, students', 48, 55-6
Questions, teacher's, 94

R

Resources, 29-32, 51-2, 91, 93, 95
Resources area, classroom, 29-30

S

Self-managing teams, 53, 71-4, 76-8
Small group work, 20
Social system of classroom, 96
Storage, classroom, 25-6
Supervised study, 53-5, 57, 59-60, 65

T

Teams 44-6, 65
Team teaching, 48
Thinking skills, 76-8, 97
Time management, 100
Tutorials, 20, 59-69

W

Whole-class teaching, 23, 33-4

Leading the Learning School *is book 15 of The School Effectiveness Series, which focuses on practical and useful ideas for individual schools and teachers. The series addresses the issues of whole school improvement along with new knowledge about teaching and learning, and offers straightforward solutions that teachers can use to make life more rewarding for themselves and those they teach.*

Book 1: *Accelerated Learning in the Classroom* by Alistair Smith
ISBN: 1855390345

- The first book in the UK to apply new knowledge about the brain to classroom practice
- Contains practical methods so teachers can apply accelerated learning theories to their own classrooms
- Aims to increase the pace of learning and deepen understanding
- Includes advice on how to create the ideal environment for learning and how to help learners fulfil their potential
- Full of lively illustrations, diagrams and plans
- Offers practical solutions on improving performance, motivation and understanding
- Contains a checklist of action points for the classroom – 21 ways to improve learning

Book 2: *Effective Learning Activities* by Chris Dickinson
ISBN: 1855390353

- An essential teaching guide which focuses on practical activities to improve learning
- Aims to improve results through effective learning, which will raise achievement, deepen understanding, promote self-esteem and improve motivation
- Includes activities which are designed to promote differentiation and understanding
- Offers advice on how to maximise the use of available – and limited – resources
- Includes activities suitable for GCSE, National Curriculum, Highers, GSVQ and GNVQ
- From the author of the highly acclaimed 'Differentiation: A Practical Handbook of Classroom Strategies'

Book 3: *Effective Heads of Department* by Phil Jones & Nick Sparks
ISBN: 1855390361

- An ideal support for Heads of Department looking to develop necessary management skills
- Contains a range of practical systems and approaches; each of the eight sections ends with a 'checklist for action'
- Designed to develop practice in line with OFSTED expectations and DfEE thinking by monitoring and improving quality
- Addresses issues such as managing resources, leadership, learning, departmental planning and making assessment valuable
- Includes useful information for Senior Managers in schools who are looking to enhance the effectiveness of their Heads of Department

Book 4: *Lessons are for Learning* by Mike Hughes
ISBN: 1855390388

- Brings together the theory of learning with the realities of the classroom environment
- Encourages teachers to reflect on their own classroom practice and challenges them to think about why they teach in the way they do
- Develops a clear picture of what constitutes effective classroom practice
- Offers practical suggestions for activities that bridge the gap between recent developments in the theory of learning and the constraints of classroom teaching
- Ideal for stimulating thought and generating discussion
- Written by a practising teacher who has also worked as a teaching advisor, a PGCE co-ordinator and an OFSTED inspector

Book 5: *Effective Learning in Science* by Paul Denley and Keith Bishop
ISBN: 1855390396
- Looks at planning for effective learning within the context of science
- Encourages discussion about the aims and purposes in teaching science and the role of subject knowledge in effective teaching
- Tackles issues such as planning for effective learning, the use of resources and other relevant management issues
- Offers help in the development of a departmental plan to revise schemes of work, resources and classroom strategies, in order to make learning and teaching more effective
- Ideal for any science department aiming to increase performance and improve results

Book 6: *Raising Boys' Achievement* by Jon Pickering
ISBN: 185539040X
- Addresses the causes of boys' underachievement and offers possible solutions
- Focuses the search for causes and solutions on teachers working in the classrooms
- Looks at examples of good practice in schools to help guide the planning and implementation of strategies to raise achievement
- Offers practical, 'real' solutions along with tried and tested training suggestions
- Ideal as a basis for INSET or as a guide to practical activities for classroom teachers

Book 7: *Effective Provision for Able & Talented Children* by Barry Teare
ISBN: 1-85539-041-8
- Basic theory, necessary procedures and turning theory into practice
- Main methods of identifying the able and talented
- Concerns about achievement and appropriate strategies to raise achievement
- The role of the classroom teacher, monitoring and evaluation techniques
- Practical enrichment activities and appropriate resources

Book 8: *Effective Careers Education & Guidance* by Andrew Edwards and Anthony Barnes
ISBN: 1-85539-045-0
- Strategic planning of the careers programme as part of the wider curriculum
- Practical consideration of managing careers education and guidance
- Practical activities for reflection and personal learning, and case studies where such activities have been used
- Aspects of guidance and counselling involved in helping students to understand their own capabilities and form career plans
- Strategies for reviewing and developing existing practice

Book 9: *Best behaviour and Best behaviour FIRST AID* by
Peter Relf, Rod Hirst, Jan Richardson and Georgina Youdell
ISBN: 1-85539-046-9
- Provides support for those who seek starting points for effective behaviour management, for individual teachers and for middle and senior managers
- Focuses on practical and useful ideas for individual schools and teachers

Best behaviour FIRST AID
ISBN: 1-85539-047-7   (pack of 5 booklets)
- Provides strategies to cope with aggression, defiance and disturbance
- Straightforward action points for self-esteem

Book 10: *The Effective School Governor* by David Marriott
    ISBN 1-85539-042-6   (including free audio tape)
- Straightforward guidance on how to fulfil a governor's role and responsibilities
- Develops your personal effectiveness as an individual governor
- Practical support on how to be an effective member of the governing team
- Audio tape for use in car or at home

Book 11: *Improving Personal Effectiveness for Managers in Schools* by James Johnson
    ISBN 1-85539-049-3
- An invaluable resource for new and experienced teachers in both primary and secondary schools
- Contains practical strategies for improving leadership and management skills
- Focuses on self-management skills, managing difficult situations, working under pressure, developing confidence, creating a team ethos and communicating effectively

Book 12: *Making Pupil Data Powerful* by Maggie Pringle and Tony Cobb
    ISBN 1-85539-052-3
- Shows teachers in primary, middle and secondary schools how to interpret pupils' performance data and how to use it to enhance teaching and learning
- Provides practical advice on analysing performance and learning behaviours, measuring progress, predicting future attainment, setting targets and ensuring continuity and progression
- Explains how to interpret national initiatives on data-analysis, benchmarking and target setting, and to ensure that these have value in the classroom

Book 13: *Closing the Learning Gap* by Mike Hughes
    ISBN 1-85539-051-5
- Helps teachers, departments and schools to close the Learning Gap between what we know about effective learning and what actually goes on in the classroom.
- Encourages teachers to reflect on the ways in which they teach, and to identify and implement strategies for improving their practice.
- Helps teachers to apply recent research findings about the brain and learning.
- Full of practical advice and real, tested strategies for improvement.
- Written by a teacher, for teachers, to stimulate thought and interest 'at a glance'.

Book 14: *Getting Started* by Henry Leibling
    ISBN 1-85539-054-X
- Provides invaluable advice for Newly Qualified Teachers (NQTs) during the three-term induction period that comprises their first year of teaching.
- Advice includes strategies on how to get to know the school and the new pupils, how to work with induction tutors, and when to ask for help.

Book 15: *Leading the Learning School* by Colin Weatherley
    ISBN 1-85539-070-1
The main theme is that the effective leadership of true 'learning schools' involves applying the principles of learning to all levels of educational management:
- Learning – 13 key principles of learning are derived from a survey of up-to-date knowledge of the brain and learning.
- Teaching – how to use the key principles of learning to improve teachers' professional knowledge and skills, make the learning environment more supportive and improve the design of learning activities.
- Staff Development – how the same principles that should underpin the design and teaching of learning activities for pupils should underpin the design and provision of development activities for teachers.
- Organizational Development – how a learning school should be consciously managed according to these same key principles of learning. The section proposes a radical new 'whole brain' approach to Development Planning.

ACCELERATED LEARNING SERIES

General Editor: **Alistair Smith**

Accelerated Learning in Practice by Alistair Smith
ISBN 1-85539-048-5

- The author's second book, which takes Nobel Prize winning brain research into the classroom.
- Structured to help readers access and retain the information necessary to begin to accelerate their own learning and that of the students they teach.
- Contains over 100 learning tools, case studies from 36 schools and an up-to-the-minute resource section
- Includes nine principles of learning based on brain research and the author's seven-stage Accelerated Learning Cycle.

The ALPS Approach: Accelerated Learning in Primary Schools
by Alistair Smith and Nicola Call
ISBN 1-85539-056-6

- Shows how research on how we learn, collected by Alistair Smith, can be used to great effect in the primary classroom.
- Provides practical and accessible examples of strategies used by highly experienced primary teacher Nicola Call, at a school where the SATs results shot up as a consequence.
- Professional, practical and exhilarating resource that gives readers the opportunity to develop the ALPS approach for themselves and for the children in their care.
- The ALPS approach includes: Exceeding expectation, 'Can-do' learning, Positive performance, Target-setting that works, Using review for recall, Preparing for tests … and much more.

MapWise by Oliver Caviglioli and Ian Harris
ISBN 1-85539-059-0

- Provides informed access to the most powerful accelerated learning technique around – Model Mapping.
- Shows how mapping can be used to address National Curriculum thinking skills requirements for students of any preferred learning style by infusing thinking into subject teaching.
- Describes how mapping can be used to measure and develop intelligence.
- Explains how mapping supports teacher explanation and student understanding.
- Demonstrates how mapping makes planning, teaching and reviewing easier and more effective.
- Written and illustrated to be lively and engaging, practical and supportive.

EDUCATION PERSONNEL MANAGEMENT SERIES

These new Education Personnel Management handbooks will help headteachers, senior managers and governors to manage a broad range of personnel issues.

The Well Teacher – management strategies for beating stress, promoting staff health and reducing absence by Maureen Cooper
ISBN 1-85539-058-2

- Provides straightforward, practical advice on how to deal strategically with staff absenteeism, which can be so expensive in terms of sick pay and supply cover, through proactively promoting staff health.
- Includes suggestions for reducing stress levels in schools.
- Outlines ways in which to deal with individual cases of staff absence.

Managing Challenging People – dealing with staff conduct by Bev Curtis and Maureen Cooper
ISBN 1-85539-057-4

- Deals with managing staff whose conduct gives cause for concern.
- Summarises the employment relationship in schools, as well as those areas of education and employment law relevant to staff discipline.
- Looks at the differences between conduct and capability, and between misconduct and gross misconduct.
- Describes disciplinary and dismissal procedures relating to teaching and non-teaching staff, including headteachers.
- Describes case studies and model procedures, and provides pro-forma letters to help schools with these difficult issues.

Managing Poor Performance – handling staff capability issues
by Bev Curtis and Maureen Cooper
ISBN 1-85539-062-0

- Explains clearly why capability is important in providing an effective and high quality education for pupils.
- Gives advice on how to identify staff with poor performance, and how to help them improve.
- Outlines the legal position and the role of governors in dealing with the difficult issues surrounding poor performance.
- Details the various stages of formal capability procedures and dismissal hearings.
- Describes case studies and model procedures, and provides pro-forma letters.

Managing Allegations Against Staff – personnel and child protection issues in schools
by Maureen Cooper
ISBN 1-85539-072-8

- Provides invaluable advice to headteachers, senior managers and personnel staff on how to deal with the difficult issues arising from accusations made against school employees.
- Shows what schools can do to protect students, while safeguarding employees from the potentially devastating consequences of false allegations.
- Describes real-life case studies.
- Provides a clear outline of the legal background plus a moral code of conduct for staff.

VISIONS OF EDUCATION SERIES

The Unfinished Revolution by John Abbott and Terry Ryan
ISBN 1-85539-064-7

- Draws on evidence from the past to show how shifting attitudes in society and politics have shaped Western education systems.
- Argues that what is now needed is a completely fresh approach, designed around evidence about how children actually learn.
- Describes a vision of an education system based on current research into how our brains work, and designed to encourage the autonomous and inventive thinkers and learners that the 21st century demands.
- Essential reading for anyone involved in education and policy making.

OTHER TITLES FROM NEP

Effective Resources for Able and Talented Children by Barry Teare
ISBN 1-85539-050-7

- A practical sequel to Barry Teare's Effective Provision for Able and Talented Children (see above), which can nevertheless be used entirely independently.
- Contains a wealth of photocopiable resources for able and talented pupils in both the primary and secondary sectors.
- Provides activities designed to inspire, motivate, challenge and stretch able children, encouraging them to enjoy their true potential.
- Resources are organised into National Curriculum areas, such as Literacy, Science and Humanities, each preceded by a commentary outlining key principles and giving general guidance for teachers.

Imagine That... by Stephen Bowkett
ISBN 1-85539-043-4

- Hands-on, user-friendly manual for stimulating creative thinking, talking and writing in the classroom.
- Provides over 100 practical and immediately useable classroom activities and games that can be used in isolation, or in combination, to help meet the requirements and standards of the National Curriculum.
- Explores the nature of creative thinking and how this can be effectively driven through an ethos of positive encouragement, mutual support and celebration of success and achievement.
- Empowers children to learn how to learn.

Self-Intelligence by Stephen Bowkett
ISBN 1-85539-055-8

- Helps explore and develop emotional resourcefulness in teachers and their pupils.
- Aims to help teachers and pupils develop the high-esteem that underpins success in education.

Helping With Reading by Anne Butterworth and Angela White
ISBN 1-85539-044-2

- Includes sections on 'Hearing Children Read', Word Recognition' and 'Phonics'.
- Provides precisely focused, easily implemented follow-up activities for pupils who need extra reinforcement of basic reading skills.
- Provides clear, practical and easily implemented activities that directly relate to the National Curriculum and 'Literacy Hour' group work. Ideas and activities can also be incorporated into Individual Education Plans.
- Aims to address current concerns about reading standards and to provide support for classroom assistants and parents helping with the teaching of reading.

Class Talk by Rosemary Sage
ISBN 1-85539-061-2

- Looks at teacher–student communication and reflects on what is happening in the classroom.
- Looks at how students talk in different classroom situations and evaluates this information in terms of planning children's learning.
- Considers the problems of transmitting meaning to others.
- Discusses and reflects on practical strategies to improve the quality of talking, teaching and learning.